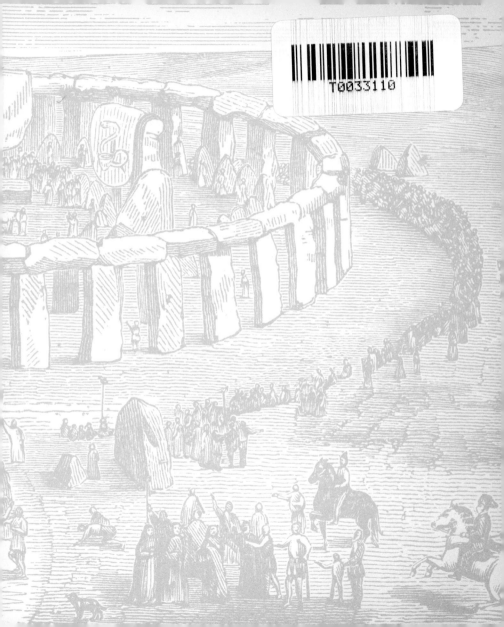

The Druid Path

STERLING ETHOS
New York

STERLING ETHOS
New York

An Imprint of Sterling Publishing Co., Inc.

STERLING ETHOS and the distinctive Sterling Ethos logo
are registered trademarks of Sterling Publishing Co., Inc.

ISBN 978-1-4549-4356-3
ISBN 978-1-4549-4357-0 (e-book)

Distributed in Canada by Sterling Publishing Co., Inc.
c/o Canadian Manda Group, 664 Annette Street
Toronto, Ontario, Canada M6S 2C8
Distributed in the United Kingdom by GMC Distribution Services
Castle Place, 166 High Street, Lewes, East Sussex, England BN7 1XU
Distributed in Australia by NewSouth Books
University of New South Wales, Sydney, NSW 2052, Australia

For information about custom editions, special sales, and premium and corporate purchases,
please contact Sterling Special Sales at 800-805-5489 or specialsales@sterlingpublishing.com.

Manufactured in China

2 4 6 8 10 9 7 5 3 1

www.sterlingpublishing.com

Design by Christine Heun
Cover design by Elizabeth Mihaltse Lindy
Picture credits—see page 203

Dedicated to the memory
of Corby Ingold,
who introduced me
to the modern Druid tradition

CONTENTS

Part Three: The Practice of Druidry

Part Four: Initiation into Druidry

INTRODUCTION

Most people these days have heard of Druids, even if the only things they know about the subject come from news photos of summer solstice celebrations at Stonehenge, the white-robed figure of Getafix in the French comic *Asterix the Gaul*, or one of the character classes in the *World of Warcraft* online roleplaying game. Even in these dim reflected forms, the image of the Druid, wise in the ways of nature, haunts the imagination of our time. What many people have never realized is that Druids exist here and now, and that Druidry—the spiritual path practiced by Druids—is an option even for those who live in a modern industrial society.

The original Druids lived many centuries ago in the Celtic countries of northwestern Europe, where Ireland, Great Britain, and France are located today. Three hundred years ago, in the early years of the Industrial Revolution, their example and the surviving records of their traditions inspired small groups of creative thinkers to begin the process of creating a Druidry for today. The movement they set in motion—the Druid Revival, as it has been called—has flourished ever since. Originally founded in England, modern Druidry spread to Europe, North America, and Australia before the nineteenth century was finished. Druids today can be found in countries all around the world.

My own introduction to Druidry happened more than a quarter century ago. In 1993, a good friend of mine introduced me to one of his friends, the late Corby Ingold, who was a Druid—a member of the Order of Bards Ovates and Druids (OBOD), then as now the largest Druid organization in the world. Corby and I hit it off immediately. After learning more about Druidry from him, I decided to join OBOD. I was initiated as a Bard by Corby and the other members of his Druid grove on May 1, 1994, and passed step by step through OBOD's distance learning program thereafter, receiving my certificate as a Druid Companion in 2002.

By then I knew that I had found my spiritual home. As the final steps of the OBOD training course drew near, I went looking for other resources to expand my knowledge and understanding of Druidry. A battered paperback on American Druid groups I found at a used bookstore mentioned another order, the Ancient Order of Druids in America (AODA) and gave an address that turned out to be outdated. When I finally managed to track down the order's secretary, I found out that AODA was clinging to existence with fewer than a dozen members, all well past retirement age. I asked to join, they accepted, conversations followed—and that was how, on the winter solstice of 2003, I became the seventh Grand Archdruid of AODA, tasked with the project of reviving an almost extinct Druid order.

The twelve years I spent thereafter as head of AODA were among the busiest and most rewarding of my life. The short version of what happened is that, with the help of many other people, I succeeded. AODA is now among the largest and most active Druid orders in the world, with members all over North America and on several other continents as well. My duties as Grand Archdruid left me very little spare time, however. It was only after I passed my office on to my successor in 2015 and settled into the much less demanding role of Archdruid Emeritus, that I had the freedom to take a broader look at modern Druidry and begin to consider other ways to share the things I have learned about the Druid tradition. This book is one of the results.

The pages before you are a portal. If you decide to pass through that portal, you will join in a quest for ancient wisdom that has been going on for three hundred years. The paths that have been marked out by the seekers who have gone before you lead past standing stones and grass-covered mounds, through deep forests and green meadows, to your own backyard and the landscape that surrounds you right now. Will you follow those paths and join in the quest? Only you can decide.

PART ONE

The Sources of Druidry

D RUIDRY IS A MODERN TRADITION OF NATURE spirituality. While its roots go back to ancient times, the history of Druidry in its present form goes back only as far as the eighteenth century. No one person founded it, nor was there a single organization that started the modern Druid movement on its way. Instead, it emerged gradually, over the course of many years, as individuals and small circles of friends began to explore the possibility of a vision of reality that embraced the presence of spirit in nature.

Is Druidry a religion? For some people, it can be. For others, it is better described as a philosophy, a practice, or a way of life. Some Druids take part in a religious tradition apart from Druidry or combine their Druidry and their religion in various ways. There have been Christian Druids, for example, since the earliest days of the modern Druid movement, and there have been Pagan Druids for just as long. Others, many of whom consider themselves spiritual but not religious, find the Druid path all by itself sufficient for their needs. What if you don't know what you believe? That's fine, too. As long as you are open to the possibility that the world is more than a random collection of lumps of dead matter in empty space, and that purpose and meaning and consciousness are present throughout the world of nature, Druidry is an option for you.

Above all else, Druidry is an orientation: a way of attending to the spiritual in natural things, of envisioning humanity as part of living nature, and of living life in relationship to the biosphere and the spiritual presences within the natural world. Each Druid expresses that orientation in a personal way. Books, teachers, and organizations can help you find your way in Druidry—that is the purpose of this book—but your own experiences and ideas are also important. If you're looking for someone to tell you what to do, Druidry is probably not a good fit for you, and if you want to tell other people what to do, then you really need to find some other option, because Druids are an independent-minded lot and will roll their eyes and walk away if you try to order them around!

To become a Druid is to take part in an adventure that has been unfolding for three hundred years, and still has unexplored regions ahead of it. The concepts, teachings, and practices given in this book are meant to help you take the first steps in your Druid journey, and the books and other resources listed at the end of this book will help you go farther.

WHITE ROBES AND GOLDEN SICKLES

When many people think of Druids, what comes to mind first is very often an image of old men in white robes carrying golden sickles to Stonehenge. The druid Getafix from the comic series *Asterix the Gaul* is a fine parody of this image, and one that many modern Druids enjoy!

The origins of this image are complicated. One of the few accounts of the ancient Druids that gives any details of their clothing and equipment describes them as wearing white robes and using a golden sickle to harvest mistletoe from oak trees. In the eighteenth century, when the Druid tradition was revived, some of the people involved in that revival took to wearing white robes in honor of the ancient Druids. Others went in their own direction. In one eighteenth-century Druid group, for example, the participants wore ordinary clothing but tied bits of colored ribbon around their right arms—the color showed how far they had proceeded in the process of studying and practicing Druidry.

Nowadays? As with so much else, it depends on the Druid. Some Druids like to wear the classic style of white robe, though I have yet to see an actual golden sickle in use among Druids. (Given the price of gold these days, one of these would be very expensive.) Others wear different colors of robes or other ceremonial garments, and plenty of Druids simply dress in ordinary clothing suited to the weather.

There are spiritual traditions that place a great deal of emphasis on having the right clothes, the right symbols, the right ritual objects, and so on. Druidry is not one of them. You can certainly equip yourself with a white robe and a sickle if that's what you want, and some modern Druid organizations and books encourage you to make or buy certain other pieces of equipment that will be useful for your Druid work, but there are only two things that are essential to study and practice Druidry: yourself and the universe you live in.

CHAPTER 1

The Ancient Druids

TO UNDERSTAND THE ROOTS OF MODERN Druidry, it helps to begin by looking into the distant past. Imagine for a moment that you were able to travel back in time more than two thousand years to ancient northwestern Europe—the regions where the countries of Ireland, Great Britain, and France are located today. The people who lived in that part of the world, back then, belonged to many small tribes and spoke variants of a common language. For food they grew wheat and barley, raised cows, pigs, and sheep, gathered nuts and wild plants from the forests, hunted wild game, and caught fish. They lived in scattered villages of houses that were dug partly into the ground to help keep them warm in winter and cool in summer. They worshiped many gods and goddesses, celebrated a complex calendar of local feasts and ceremonies, and loved music, poetry, and stories.

They fought among themselves, their chieftains riding chariots pulled by ponies, their young men on foot with spears, swords, and big shields. The great discoveries that were already reshaping life in distant lands farther south and east—writing, cities, and more—had not yet reached them. They were the ancient Celts, and it was among them that the Druids first appeared.

No one knows where that first and oldest version of Druidry came from. It might have been created by the ancient Celts themselves. It might have been passed down from the people who lived in those lands before the Celts got there, the forgotten nations that built Stonehenge and the other stone circles of those lands. It might have come from somewhere else. We simply don't know. What we do know is that when travelers from Greece and Rome reached the Celtic lands of northwestern Europe, living among the tribal peoples there, they found Druids: men and women who devoted their lives to wisdom.

These Druids *knew* the powers of herbs and stones and the rhythms of planets and stars. They composed poems, recited myths and tribal histories, and passed on wisdom teachings to those who wanted to learn from them. The Druids weren't priests and priestesses—the travelers who came to the Celtic lands had plenty of priests and priestesses back home and never used those terms for the Druids. The name these seekers of wisdom used for themselves probably meant "wise ones of the oaks" in the Welsh language, which is descended from the ancient Celtic tongue; "druid" is *derwydd*, from *derw*, "oak," and *gwydd* (*-wydd* when combined with another word), is an old term for wisdom or knowledge.

Young men and women who wanted to become Druids went to study with an experienced Druid. Since none of the Druid teachings were ever written down, all of it had to be memorized, and it took some students

twenty years to learn everything they needed to know to become Druids. Once they completed their studies, they no longer took part in tribal warfare, and they devoted their time to teaching and to their other duties as Druids. Some married and raised families, while others did not. The wisest and most learned Druids often became advisers to kings, but many others lived much humbler lives: living and working in a single small village, teaching children, healing the sick, and performing ceremonies for the people.

That was how things were when the Romans began their campaigns of conquest in northwestern Europe. The Celtic warriors fought bravely, but Roman military technology and organization made it a hopeless fight. During the long struggle, Druids took a leading role in coordinating the resistance, and the Romans responded by outlawing Druidry and killing a great many Druids. In the countries that Rome conquered—today's France, Brittany, England, and Wales—Druids survived only in secret, and many of them had to find other ways to support themselves; centuries after the conquest, one Roman writer mentions a Druid who worked as an innkeeper. In the Celtic lands that stayed outside Rome's grasp—today's Scotland and Ireland—Druids remained active for centuries longer.

What finally put an end to the ancient Druids was the coming of Christianity. Elsewhere in the ancient world, Christians and Pagans went after each other in waves of violent persecution. While very little of that ever took place in ancient Scotland and Ireland, Christian missionaries who came to those lands had learned to distrust all spiritual traditions outside their own churches. Gradually, under pressure from Celtic tribal chieftains, the Christian clergy and the Druids worked out a wary compromise. Those Druids who didn't become Christian priests, monks, and nuns, as some did, became bards instead, using their knowledge of myths and tribal histories and their skill with poetic verse to support themselves and preserve some of their traditions. Over the generations that followed, while the legends of the Celts were preserved by the bards, most of the other teachings of Druidry were lost, and the Druids themselves became a fading memory. More than a thousand years would pass before Druids would emerge again from the realms of legend.

MISTLETOE

One of the most detailed descriptions of the ancient Druids comes from the Roman writer Pliny the Elder, who put an account of a Druid ceremony in the pages of his book *Natural History*. According to Pliny, the Druids considered mistletoe, a parasitic plant that grows on trees, a holy healing plant. They believed it was especially sacred and medicinally effective when it appeared on an oak, which happened very rarely in Europe.

When an oak with mistletoe growing on it was discovered, Druids dressed in white robes would come to harvest it on the sixth day after the new moon. One Druid would climb up the oak to where the mistletoe grew, carrying a golden sickle to cut the plant, while others on the ground below would hold a white cloth stretched out underneath the tree to catch the mistletoe when it fell. Once it was harvested, two bullocks would be sacrificed to the Celtic gods, and their meat roasted and shared in a community celebration, for the Druids knew how to make a medicine from mistletoe that, as Pliny wrote, could cure all diseases.

Pliny got at least one detail of the ceremony wrong, for gold is a very soft metal and a sickle made of gold won't cut cardboard, much less the tough stem of a mistletoe plant. The ancient Celts were skilled blacksmiths, however, and it would have been easy for them to make a sickle of steel and then put a thin layer of gilding on the blade, except for the cutting edge, so that it would look like gold. What else Pliny might have gotten wrong, we have no way of knowing, but his account of the ceremony became a source of inspiration for the Druid Revival, when it began many centuries later.

STONEHENGE

Nobody knows whether the ancient Druids had anything to do with Stonehenge, the famous ring of standing stones on England's Salisbury Plain. Archeologists these days believe that the first Celtic peoples came to Britain sometime after 1300 BCE, and Stonehenge was built in several phases, the earliest beginning around 2950 BCE and the latest ending around 1600 BCE. If the ancient Druids originated among the Celts, they had nothing to do with Stonehenge. If, on the other hand, ancient Druidry had its roots in surviving traditions from the age of the stone circles and was passed on to the Celts after they arrived in northwestern Europe, then it makes sense to say that the ancient Druids were descended from the builders of Stonehenge. Since the origins of the ancient Druids are unknown, we simply can't say.

What we know for certain is that Stonehenge and other megalithic structures played an important role in shaping the modern Druid movement that began in the eighteenth century. Visit any of the old stone circles and you'll find, as countless Druids have done through the years, that while most churches and other religious structures shut out the world, standing stones direct your attention to the surrounding landscape and the sky above. That experience helped encourage the people who revived the tradition to make Druidry a spiritual path rooted in living nature. It is an important reason why Druids began celebrating their rituals in stone circles, almost

as soon as the Druid Revival got started and explains why they began to welcome the summer solstice at Stonehenge as soon as they could get the legal right to do so.

Some archeologists like to insist that there's something wrong with that explanation, but what they've forgotten is that the history of Stonehenge as a sacred place did not end in 1600 BCE. It remains a sacred place today for Druids around the world, and for many others who may not call themselves Druids but who recognize that standing beneath the open sky, surrounded by the mighty stones raised by the ancients, can be as moving and transformative an experience today as it was before the first Celt set foot on Britain's shores.

CELTIC LEGENDS

Among the legacies that remain from the days of the ancient Celts are collections of legends that were written down in the Middle Ages. Most of those survived in Ireland, where Druids lasted longer than anywhere else and where Christian monks took pride in the legends of their ancestors and copied down the old stories into handwritten books. Three great cycles of those tales come from Ireland: the Mythological Cycle, which chronicles the settlement of Ireland by many groups of settlers and their gods; the Ulster Cycle, which tells the stories of the hero Cuchulain and the warriors of the Red Branch; and the Fenian Cycle, which collects the stories of the warrior chieftain Fionn mac Cumhaill and his companions.

From Wales come the *Four Branches of the Mabinogi*—four tales of magic set before the Roman conquest—and a handful of other ancient stories. Wales and Brittany also kept a far more extensive tradition alive, however. In both countries, folktales about a war leader of the early Middle Ages were enriched with a great deal of much older material, dating far back into the Celtic past. In the twelfth century, Welsh and Breton storytellers recounted these tales to eager listeners in France and England, recasting them in terms of the knightly culture of the time. The war leader turned into King Arthur, his warriors were reframed as the knights of the Round Table, and the Arthurian legends became one of the great storehouses of Celtic lore and legend, under a thin layer of medieval imagery.

Many Druids today study these legends to deepen their understanding of Druidry's Celtic roots. Don't make the mistake of thinking of them as holy scriptures, however! The closest modern Druids have to scriptures is the natural world itself, which constantly teaches wisdom to those who pay close attention to it. The legends of the ancient Celtic peoples are there to be studied, reflected on, and above all else, enjoyed.

CHAPTER 2

The Druid Revival

IN THE EARLY YEARS OF THE EIGHTEENTH century, many people in Great Britain were dissatisfied with the spiritual options that their culture offered them. On the one hand, the churches of the time offered a cold and rationalistic Christianity that replaced personal spiritual experience with blind belief in formal doctrines and obedience to the established social order. On the other, supporters of the newly launched movement of scientific materialism insisted that spirituality was nonsense, and nothing existed but dead matter and the void. Faced with a choice between those two options, some people decided to look for a third choice—and one of the things they found was the legend of the ancient Druids.

British historians by then had already gathered up everything that the Greek and Roman writers had to say about the Druids of their time and had begun to study the old Irish lore about Druids. That made it easy for people in the eighteenth century to envision a tradition similar to that of the ancient Druids but adapted for the needs of their own time. The idea of a nature spirituality practiced beneath the open sky, recognizing the presence of spirit in the phenomena of nature, was also profoundly appealing to people who had already begun to see the environmental destruction caused by the first waves of the Industrial Revolution. Even though the secrets of the ancient Druids were lost forever, some of these eighteenth-century spiritual rebels decided to take the same name for themselves and set out to recover or reinvent something like the traditions of the Druids of ancient times. The movement they founded thus came to be called the Druid Revival.

No one knows exactly when the Druid Revival began. Certain traditions in today's Druid movement claim that the first Druid organization of modern times was founded in 1717, though no one has yet found solid proof of this. By the 1740s, certainly, the Rev. William Stukeley, an influential early Druid, was holding meetings of an informal Druid society at his home in London, and by the end of the century Druid groups had been founded in various parts of England, Wales, Ireland, and the newly founded United States of America, where the Society of Ancient Druids was organized in New York State in 1798. Though the Druid movement was small and scattered in those early days, it laid down foundations on which generations of future Druids would build.

It also established a tradition that would be central to Druidry ever after: a refusal to burden the movement with dogma and hierarchy.

That tradition became central to the Revival partly by circumstances, for its early members had many different views about spirituality. From the very beginning there were Christian Druids, Pagan Druids, and pantheist Druids, all of whom somehow managed to get along most of the time. They had also gotten past the habit of thinking that spirituality required belief in a specific set of opinions or obedience to this or that authority figure and helped Druidry emerge in its modern form as a personal encounter with the presence of spirit in nature.

That same vision helped the Revival deal with the most important challenge that it faced: the need to create new traditions of teaching and practice. Since the teachings of the ancient Druids had been lost a thousand years before, the new Druids of the eighteenth century had very little to work with at first. Scraps of Celtic tradition preserved in old Welsh and Irish literature, borrowings from other spiritual traditions, and personal experience provided the raw materials. Over time, though, various Druid groups and individuals pieced together symbols, rituals, and methods of spiritual practice, and those that worked well were further refined over generations. The resulting openness to innovation and experimentation became a source of strength for the movement.

New spiritual movements come and go, but the Druid Revival had staying power. All through the nineteenth and twentieth centuries, Druid organizations of various kinds spread through Europe, North America, Australia, and New Zealand. Some of them, especially in Celtic countries such as Wales and Brittany, focused their efforts on reviving and preserving Celtic languages, culture, and literature. Some became cooperative societies that helped people work together and weather the challenges of life. Some performed elaborate public ceremonies at sacred sites such as

Stonehenge and Glastonbury, while others met privately in secluded places in the woods. Since the Druid community made ample room for variation and creativity, all these and more helped enrich the traditions of Druidry and opened the doors to further exploration in the years ahead.

PYTHAGORAS AND THE DRUIDS

When the founders of the Druid Revival began constructing a modern nature spirituality, some of the most important resources were the accounts

of ancient Druids written down by Greek and Roman scholars more than fifteen centuries earlier. None of those accounts set out a complete system of Druid teaching, or anything like one, but they included hints of great value. One of those hints, made by several Greek writers, implied that Druid teachings were similar to those of the Greek philosopher Pythagoras.

Born in 570 BCE, Pythagoras traveled the world in search of wisdom, and founded a school in the city of Crotona, now known as Crotone, Italy. Most people nowadays remember Pythagoras for his discoveries in the field of what is now geometry, but he was not just a mathematician. He claimed to remember his own past lives and taught a system of spirituality that included sacred geometry, astronomy, and music as subjects for meditation and ways to train the mind. Like the ancient Druids, he left no writings, but later on, students of what came to be called the Pythagorean tradition wrote their own accounts of his teachings.

Those Pythagorean writings were more than enough to inspire modern Druids to explore and borrow freely from them. Druids interested in Stonehenge and other ancient sites have worked out the geometry by which those sites were built and have practiced forms of mental training modeled on Pythagoras's system. More generally, the journeys Pythagoras made on his quest for wisdom inspired many Druids to learn about other spiritual teachings and traditions and draw inspiration from those sources to enrich Druidry.

WILLIAM STUKELEY'S ELEPHANTS

One of the most influential of the early Druids was Rev. William Stukeley. Born in 1687, he became one of Britain's first archeologists as well as a minister in the Anglican Church. His books on the stone circles at Stonehenge and Avebury contain plenty of Druid philosophy. He was one of the founders of Christian Druidry, and he also helped set in motion another tradition that spread just as widely through the Druid Revival: a tradition of deadpan humor.

The historians of Stukeley's time believed that the ancient inhabitants of Britain were howling, ignorant savages, and so came up with a flurry of theories insisting that Stonehenge must have been built by the Romans, the Vikings, the Phoenicians—anybody, in fact, except the people who were there at the time. Stukeley set out to poke fun at these theories by putting a chapter in his book on Stonehenge insisting that the stone circle had been built by intelligent elephants from Africa and borrowed all the arguments of the historians to prop up his deliberately silly theory. It was great satire, though some people still don't get the joke.

Stukeley was far from the only influential Druid to engage in this kind of humor. In the early nineteenth century, for example, some historians believed that the oldest religion in the world—founded by the survivors of Noah's flood—used the Sun and Noah's ark as central religious symbols. This Helio-Arkite faith was promptly and merrily adopted by Druids, who used it as a way to make fun of attacks from the more intolerant Christian ministers of their time. After all, as good Helio-Arkites, they could afford to roll their eyes at Johnny-come-latelies like the Presbyterians and Baptists!

THE BARD OF GLAMORGAN

His real name was Edward Williams, and he was a construction worker by trade, but he became one of the great figures of the Druid Revival under the pen name Iolo Morganwg. Born in 1747 in the county of Glamorgan in southern Wales, Iolo was fluent in Welsh from earliest childhood, and in his teen years learned the art of traditional Welsh poetry from some of the last of the old Welsh bards. As an adult he went to London and tried to make a career as a poet, with little success. So few people were interested in his poetry that he ended up forging medieval Welsh poems and claiming he'd found them in Wales just to find an audience. (His forgeries were very skillfully done; some of his fakes weren't identified as his work until the 1950s).

Some people achieve their most improbable dreams after many failures, and that was Iolo's fate. Having failed to launch a literary career, he tried his hand at shopkeeping and then at farming, with no better luck. All the while, he brooded on the great days of the past, when the Welsh bards were honored by aristocrats. Eventually, his dreams took over his life; he proclaimed himself the heir of the bards of old Glamorgan and started acting accordingly, holding gatherings to enroll students and teach the secrets of the Welsh bards to those who qualified for them.

Astonishingly, that was when the success that had eluded him for so many years came to him at last. For thirty years, supported by friends and admirers, he traveled through Wales, founding *gorseddau* (bardic assemblies) and calling on Welsh poets to return to the traditions of the old bards—traditions that Iolo himself had mostly invented. The poets, and a great many others, responded enthusiastically. His efforts helped spark a major revival of Welsh poetry, culture, and language, and also spread all through the Druid Revival. To this day, if you attend a Druid ceremony, the odds are good that some elements of that ceremony came from Iolo Morganwg's quest to revive Welsh bardism.

CHAPTER 3

Druids Today

TODAY DRUIDRY IS THRIVING. THOUGH THEY get little attention from the mass media, Druids can be found all through Europe, North America, Australia, and New Zealand, and in some parts of Asia and South America. When historian of Druidry Michel Raoult set out to calculate the size of the Druid movement in the early 1980s—the only census of modern Druids ever attempted—his best estimate was that there were between one and two million Druids worldwide. Given the steady growth in the tradition in recent years, the upper end of that estimate is probably close to accurate today.

The history of Druidry in recent times has been complicated by the rise of Neopagan religions such as Wicca. As noted on pages 34–35, Druidry and Wicca are not the same thing, and Druidry isn't part of the Neopagan movement—the Druid Revival was a going concern, after all, more than two centuries before the emergence of the first Neopagan religions after the Second World War. Relations between Druids and Neopagans have sometimes been difficult, because certain Neopagan groups have promoted themselves as the exclusive heirs of ancient Celtic spirituality and denounce Druidry in overheated language. Others have taken a more constructive approach and explore the common ground between Druidry and Neopaganism. As a result, some Neopagan groups have borrowed elements of Druid Revival teaching and practice, while some Druid groups have also found elements of Neopaganism to their taste.

Today those who like to participate in Druid organizations have plenty of choices. The largest Druid organization in the world today, the Order of Bards Ovates and Druids (OBOD), was founded in 1964 by Ross Nichols, an English poet and educator who was trained and initiated in another Druid order and then left to pursue his own vision. While the OBOD fell into abeyance after Nichols's death in 1974, it was revived ten years later by Philip Carr-Gomm, who launched what has proved to be an extremely popular distance learning program. That program and Carr-Gomm's many books on Druidry played a key role in the growth of Druidry all around the world in the years that followed.

Another Druid order that underwent a comparable revival was the Ancient Order of Druids in America (AODA), founded in 1912 by a group of American Druids, chartered by a British Druid organization. Like most small spiritual groups, AODA had its ups and downs. At the beginning of the twenty-first century, it was on the brink of extinction, but in 2003 it elected a new Grand Archdruid. As mentioned in the introduction, that event initiated a period of steady growth, which continues to this day. Meanwhile new organizations such as the Druid Network have also emerged and provide other venues for Druids to contact one another and learn more about the tradition.

For every Druid who belongs to an organization of this kind, however, there are many who belong to a smaller, local Druid group—often consisting of an informal group of friends who share an interest in nature spirituality—or simply practice Druidry on their own. The growth of solitary Druidry, sparked first by OBOD's distance learning program, then by the publication of many good books on the subject, and finally by the appearance of Druid teachings on the internet, has been one of the most striking changes in the movement in recent years. This book, as you have already probably guessed, is meant to provide solitary Druids and small, local Druid groups with teachings and practices that will help deepen their understanding of Druidry and their relationship with nature and the spiritual powers within nature.

As we move farther into the twenty-first century, reframing humanity's relationship with nature and spirit has become one of the foremost requirements of our time. The environmental impact of the Industrial Revolution, which helped launch the Druid Revival three centuries ago, has spread around the world since that time and set in motion a crisis that now affects us all. Attempts to address that crisis from a purely materialistic stance, without drawing on the power and inspiration of the spiritual realm, have accomplished little. Many spiritual traditions have important gifts to offer in this time of great danger and great possibility, but Druidry's focus on nature spirituality, in particular, responds to needs that so many people feel today. This book is meant to help them find what they are looking for.

DRUIDRY AND WICCA

Some people these days confuse Druidry with the Neopagan religion of Wicca. There's a certain amount of history to that confusion, because Gerald Gardner, the person who first publicized Wicca, was a close friend of Ross Nichols, one of the most influential figures in twentieth-century Druidry, and the two shared many interests and ideas. They also shared a ceremonial sword. For a while in the 1950s, Gardner and Nichols made sure to schedule rituals on different days, so that there would be no conflict over who got to use the sword!

Wicca and Druidry are not the same thing, however. Wicca is a religion, worshipping its own goddess and god. It has its own sacred writing, the Book of Shadows, which varies from one Wiccan tradition to another. It has its own distinctive ceremonies, customs, symbols, and jargon, which are not the same as the ones that Druids use. Pentagrams, athames (ceremonial daggers), ritual nudity, sabbats, cakes and ale, casting a circle, and calling the quarters—all these belong to Wicca, not to Druidry.

Does that mean that if you happen to be a Wiccan, you can't practice Druidry? Not at all. One of the things that sets Druidry apart from many other spiritual traditions is that it's not exclusive, and all who want to participate may do so, provided that they show respect for the traditions of Druidry and don't try to force their beliefs or practices onto others. Here, as so often in life, ordinary courtesy and a willingness to learn new things will take care of most problems.

DRUIDRY AND THE ENVIRONMENT

Since the origins of the Druid Revival in the eighteenth century, Druids have been attentive to the problems created by humanity's careless mistreatment of the natural world. Many people nowadays have forgotten that air pollution was a serious problem in many cities in Europe by 1800, and coal mines and factory districts were blighting the landscape even before then. That concern remains an important theme in Druidry today, when there are so many more

people in the world than there were in 1800, and the number and variety of pollutants have increased even faster than the population.

Central to the Druid approach to these issues, however, is the recognition that care for the environment has to start with the individual. One of the main reasons the environmental crisis has become so serious despite decades of activism is that too many people want someone else to stop polluting while refusing to make any changes to their own lifestyles. Druids focus instead on taking responsibility for their own contributions to the problem, decreasing their ecological footprints and supporting programs to plant trees, restore habitats, and the like. In this as in other contexts, Druids see personal example as the most effective form of leadership.

A quote apocryphally attributed to Mahatma Gandi is: "You must be the change you wish to see in the world." You don't have to change your life all at once, and in fact it usually works better to start small, with one or two simple changes. Replacing toxic cleaning supplies with natural ones or putting on a sweater instead of turning up the thermostat in winter may not seem like much, but these and changes like them make a measurable difference, and they develop the habit of personal ecological responsibility—a habit that can become the basis for bigger changes later on.

WOMEN IN DRUIDRY

Now and again books have promoted the mistaken idea that Druidry is only for men. That has never been true. Back in the days of the ancient Celts, women as well as men studied the traditional teachings and became Druids. The Druid Revival, inspired by this, encouraged women to take on active roles in the movement from the eighteenth century onward. Today, there are roughly as many women involved in the modern Druid movement as there are men. As I write this, two of the Druid organizations mentioned in this book, OBOD and AODA, are both headed by women, and women have an active and honored role in many other Druid organizations and activities.

No great fuss is made about such things in Druidry, for a simple yet subtle reason: gender is not especially important in Druid thought and practice. Some religious and spiritual traditions place a great deal of stress on gender. In many forms of Wicca, for example, the gender of the Wiccan deities, the Goddess and the God, is of central importance. In many other religions, certain roles such as priesthood are only open to one gender.

Druidry is different. In Druidry, the relationship that matters most is between the individual human being and the world of nature. That simply isn't a relationship where gender matters much. In the same way, other common lines of division among human beings, such as skin color and ethnicity, are considered irrelevant by Druids. As human beings we all stand in the same relationship to nature and the spiritual powers that act through nature. That common ground outweighs the various factors that might otherwise divide us.

PART TWO

THE
WISDOM
OF
DRUIDRY

ACCORDING TO THE TRAVELERS WHO MET THEM and wrote about them, the ancient Druids were devoted to the quest for wisdom. What they discovered in their explorations we will probably never know, but their example inspired the founders of the Druid Revival to take up the same quest. Three hundred years later, modern Druids have inherited a substantial body of traditions, teachings, and lore from their predecessors on the Druid path.

To make sense of this heritage, it's important to remember the difference between wisdom and knowledge. You can know an enormous amount and not be wise, and you can be wise without having vast amounts of knowledge. Most of the problems society faces today, in fact, come out of the fact that we have too much knowledge and not enough wisdom!

Wisdom can be defined as a sense of meaningful patterns. All through the world, as we experience it, things happen according to ever-repeating patterns and rhythms, and if you recognize these, you can anticipate what will happen and what you should do in response. For example, everything made of matter has a life cycle; things are born, they develop, they mature, they grow old, and they die. If you learn to watch for that pattern, you can very often tell where something is in its life cycle and tell the difference between something that looks weak because it's at the beginning of its life cycle and has a great deal of growing ahead of it, and something that looks weak because it's at the end of its life cycle and is fading out of existence.

Like the concept of a life cycle, ways of finding meaningful patterns in our experience of the world and in ourselves are central to the teachings of Druidry. They are tools for thinking, rather than facts about the world that must be memorized or looked up. They are traditionally passed on in symbolic form because this makes them easier to learn, and because it also makes it less likely that people will miss the point and think of them as facts rather than tools for thinking. As you read the pages that follow, keep that distinction in mind. Ask yourself questions like these: what patterns are these symbols trying to teach me? Where do I see those patterns in the world around me and in myself? Are there ways those patterns might be useful to me, to help make more sense of things that I find confusing or random?

The teachings of Druidry are among the places where Druidry comes closest to religion because religions are (among other things) immense collections of traditional wisdom. Whatever else the symbols and stories of religions may also be, they are ways of passing on the sense of meaningful patterns to believers. This is one of the reasons why many religious people study the scriptures and sacred stories of their faith, and it's also one of the reasons why many Druids study the myths and legends of the ancients as part of their quest for wisdom. The practice of Druidic meditation, which is discussed in chapter 9, is among other things a way to understand the patterns woven into the stories and symbols of the past.

DRUIDRY AND RELIGION

Ever since the early days of the Druid Revival, some Druids have been active participants in churches and other religious bodies, while others have not. Over the years, Druids have created forms of Druidry oriented toward certain religious options, so that in today's Druid movement you will sometimes hear people discussing Christian Druidry, Pagan Druidry, and so on. If you follow a particular faith, you can certainly draw on these forms as you find your own Druid path and combine the insights of your faith with those of the Druid tradition, as many Druids have done before you.

PANTHEIST DRUIDRY also dates back to the beginning of the Revival—in fact, John Toland, the first influential pantheist in the English-speaking world, is honored as a founding member of some of today's Druid traditions. Pantheists do not believe in a personal God but see nature itself as an impersonal divine unity. Every material thing, in their view, is part of the body of God, and every living being a cell in the divine mind.

CHRISTIAN DRUIDRY dates back to the very beginnings of the Druid Revival. William Stukeley, one of the most important figures in the eighteenth-century Druid movement, was an Anglican minister, and many Druids since his time have been members or clergy in many different Christian churches. Christian Druids remember that the first chapter of the Gospel of John teaches that the world of nature was created by Jesus Christ—"All things were made by Him, and without Him was not any thing made that was made"—and therefore see nature as the oldest Gospel, the first revelation of the divine nature to created beings.

PAGAN DRUIDRY is another long-established Druid tradition, going back to the first eighteenth-century attempts to recover the religious traditions of the ancient Celtic peoples. Pagan Druidry is polytheistic—that is, like the ancient Celts, it recognizes and worships many gods and goddesses, who each govern one or more of the forces of nature—and it draws religious inspiration from what remains today of the myths, legends, and traditions of ancient Celtic spirituality.

Are these the only options? Of course not. There are also Jewish Druids, Buddhist Druids, Hindu Druids, and so on. If you follow one of these religious traditions, or some other, and also decide to take up the Druid path, close study of the scriptures and traditions of your own faith along with the teachings of Druidry will help you find the best way to proceed. On the other hand, if you are uncomfortable with religion or simply don't find it relevant to you, you can practice Druidry by itself without taking up any of these options.

CHAPTER 4

The
One Life

MYSTICS, VISIONARIES, HEALERS, AND STUDENTS of ancient lore around the world and across the ages have taught that life is not simply an accidental chemical process that is present in certain things and absent in everything else. Life, from their perspective, is a force that exists everywhere and in all things, whether or not those things seem to be alive from a human perspective. This life force has had countless names in the different languages of the world. Martial artists and Buddhist monks in Japan call it *ki*, while their equivalents in China call it *qi*. Yogis in India call it *prana*. In the Hebrew Bible, it is called *ruach*, and in the Greek of the New Testament its name is *pneuma*. Many Druids use the old Welsh word for it and call it *nwyfre* (pronounced "NOO-iv-ruh"). In this book, we will call it by another common Druid term, the One Life.

Ideas like this one make a difference. Think of everything in the world as full of life, woven together into a unity by the flowing currents of nwyfre, and your experience of the world is not the same as it would be if you think of the world as a vast lifeless void in which scattered lumps of dead matter drift around at random. That second way of thinking of things is fashionable right now among some scientists, but even today there are some researchers who suggest that it's an inaccurate view, and that the scientists of the future will find their way back to the traditional vision of life as a force that flows through everything in the universe.

Take a moment now, as you are reading this, to enter into the traditional way of thinking about the world. Imagine the life force flowing through everything around you, and through you as well. Feel it surging into you, when you breathe in, and flowing gently back out of you, when you breathe out. Think of every atom of matter around you as being held in place by a lattice of life force, and of yourself as a part of that life force, one with the One Life. That is how Druids experience the world. As you work with the practices of the Druid path, you will find that this way of experiencing things becomes natural and easy for you.

Everything in the world manifests the One Life in different ways. In stone, the One Life expresses itself as solidity; in running water, as flow; in the wind, as movement; in the sun, as light and heat. Plants and trees express the One Life in growth and form, animals in activity and awareness; every kind of plant and animal does so in its own unique way. Get to know the different kinds of trees that grow where you live, and you will become aware of the way that each one grows, moves, and adapts to the cycle of the seasons; learn to watch the animals and birds that live near you, and you will become aware of the way that each moves and

acts and responds to the things it encounters. All these are expressions of the One Life.

Human beings, too, have their own unique expression of the One Life. In Druid tradition this is called Awen (pronounced "AH-wen"), the spirit of creativity and inspiration. The ability to imagine, to innovate, and to create is the distinct way that the One Life expresses itself in us. This sets us apart from other living things, but it also makes us distinct from each other, for every person's Awen is at least a little different from everyone else's. Some Druids take up music, dance, writing, or some other art form as a way to express their personal Awen. Another art is even more important, however, and this is the art of everyday life.

THE DRUID WAY OF LIFE

Many spiritual traditions have long lists of rules and commandments, which are meant to tell their followers how to live their lives. From the beginnings of the Revival, Druidry has taken a different approach. Since each person's Awen is at least a little different from everyone else's, no two people can live exactly the same life or follow exactly the same set of rules. At the heart of the Druid way of life, accordingly, is the quest to find and follow your own Awen: to figure out what life you are meant to lead, what inspiration calls to you, what forms of creativity appeal to you, and then to live the life, follow the inspiration, and express the creativity that is your unique calling in the world.

This isn't easy. Every human society sets up rules, customs, and habits with an eye toward what works for most people most of the time. If you choose to follow your own Awen you'll inevitably come into conflict with other people's habits and expectations at least some of the time. Since they have just as much right to follow their Awen as you have to follow yours, you can't make them behave the way you want, or think the way you want. All you can do is live your own life in a way that avoids conflict where possible and accept the fact that some people are never going to understand why you choose to do what you do.

In the same way, remember that what works for you may not work for other people. Some Druid teachers make this point by talking about the Druid diet. The Druid diet? It consists of figuring out which foods make you feel healthy and happy, and eating a diet based on those foods. Your body is at least a little different from every other human body in the world, and the diet that keeps it well-nourished may not be a suitable diet for anyone but you.

This approach doubtless seems strange, in an era when so many people seem to be obsessed with telling everyone else what to do with their lives, but it's the Druid way. Try finding and following your own Awen and letting other people make their own choices, and you'll find that it really does make life better for everyone.

RECOGNIZING THE ONE LIFE
IN ALL THINGS

We are all always in contact with the One Life, since it sustains our very existence, but it's possible to be more or less conscious of that contact. Druids practice to become more mindful of their connection to the life that is present in all things. There are many ways to do this, and indeed Druidry as a whole can be seen as a way of recognizing and honoring our relationship with the One Life.

All the ways you relate to the world of nature around you are, among other things, ways that you are in contact with the One Life. The air that you breathe, the water that you drink, the food that you eat, the material things that you interact with, and above all, the living things, human and otherwise, that are part of your life—all of these are forms taken by the life force as it flows through the universe, as are your own body and mind and spirit. How you deal with these forms is part of how you interact with the One Life.

One way that many Druids acknowledge their connection with the One Life is the practice of gratitude. At least once each day, and more often if you feel inspired to do so, let yourself be grateful for everything in the world that sustains your life. Take a few moments to think about all the things, great and small, that make it possible for you to live and thrive. Be thankful that they are there for you, and be thankful for the cycles and processes of nature that put them there. If you take the time to learn a little about how nature works, this practice becomes more vivid and meaningful: once you know that every drop of water you use for drinking, washing, or any other purpose was lifted up from some distant ocean by sunlight, fell as rain or snow, and flowed through the world above or below the surface of the ground before it was gathered by a pipe and brought to your tap, your experience of water becomes a participation in one of the great cycles of nature.

The practice of gratitude is especially important when dealing with food. Everything you eat was once a living being who gave its life so that you can live. This dependence on other lives is true of all living things, not just you: all life lives on life and shares its life with other living things. With every bite of food you eat, you are taking part in the pattern in the One Life that ecologists call the food web. Take a moment before each meal to be thankful for all the lives that helped support your life. If you want that moment of gratitude to take the traditional form of saying grace—whether that involves expressing your thoughts and feelings of the moment or reciting the words of a familiar prayer before meals—that's certainly an option.

More generally, Druids recognize that they do not live separate, isolated lives. Each of us has our own Awen, our own unique purpose and path in life, but every individual Awen is one note in the symphony of existence. In the final analysis, everything and every being in the whole universe is a unique individual expression of the One Life. Recognize this and act accordingly, and you will find that the world becomes a more magical place for you.

CHAPTER 5

The Two
Currents

THE ONE LIFE FLOWS THROUGH ALL THINGS
and takes many forms in the world of nature around
us, but two of those forms have special importance
in Druidry. The sun and the earth are the two most
potent expressions of the One Life in the world, and so
they are the great sources of power in Druid ritual and
spiritual practice. In many Druid traditions the flow of
the One Life from the sun is simply referred to as the
solar current, and the flow from deep within the earth is
called the telluric current, from Tellus, an old word for
the earth. These two currents cycle constantly through
everything on earth. When they are in balance, life
flourishes. When they are out of balance, life is out of
balance, and troubles follow.

The solar current flows out from the center of
the sun and streams through space, descending to the
earth's surface from above. It is stronger, of course,

when the sun is above the horizon, which is why some Druid rituals are traditionally practiced "in the face of the sun, the eye of light"—that is to say, outdoors in the daytime, with the sun shining down on the ritual. In the course of the day, it is strongest at dawn and at noon. It also varies over the course of the year, reaching its greatest strength on the day of the summer solstice (June 22 in the Northern Hemisphere) and its least strength on the day of the winter solstice (December 21 in the Northern Hemisphere). Because it waxes and wanes across the cycles of day and year, many Druids think of it as the current of time. Because its effects are particularly strong on mind and consciousness, it is also called the current of knowledge.

The telluric current flows out from the core of the earth and streams through the mantle and the crust, rising up to the earth's surface from below. Because its effects are particularly strong on health and vigor, it is called the current of power. Where the solar current is the current of time, the telluric current is also the current of place: it is stronger in some places than others and takes on different qualities from the stone and soil through which it flows. Ancient sacred sites are always located in places where the telluric current is strong and beneficial, but even where there are no old sacred places, or where their locations have been lost, spots where the telluric current is strong can be found by those who know how. Natural springs, where water flows up from underground, mark sites where the telluric current wells up along with the water, and big, healthy trees also show where the telluric current is strong.

Trees have another lesson to teach about the two currents. Most trees taper as they go up: their trunks are thickest close to the ground, and the higher they reach, the finer and more delicate they become. If you look at your own body, you can see the same pattern turned upside down! Your arms and legs become finer and more delicate as they descend toward the ground. Trees have their hair at the bottom—we call those hairs "roots"—while you have yours at the top. You are an inverted tree, and a tree is an inverted human.

In Druid tradition, this difference comes out of the relationship that humans and trees have to the two currents. Trees, and plants more generally, are channels for the telluric current, drawing it up from underground and letting it flow out through the atmosphere into space. Humans,

and animals more generally, are channels for the solar current, bringing it down from the sky and letting it flow through soil and stone into the depths of the earth. Humans and trees balance each other. This is why nowadays, when there are so many human beings and not enough trees in the world, many Druids make a point of planting trees whenever they can. Scientists can tell you that trees breathe in the carbon dioxide we breathe out, and breathe out the oxygen we breathe in. This is true, but Druids know that the partnership between humans and trees goes further than this, into the mysterious balance of the two currents.

STANDING STONES AND SACRED WELLS

In some parts of the world, many centuries ago, people learned how to tap into the solar and telluric currents to help bring fertility to crops and herds. Like most ancient peoples, they paid close attention to subtle changes in their surroundings, and the things that they observed taught them things that scientists today are only just beginning to learn. The secret lore of the two currents is among these lost secrets of the ancient world.

The forgotten art of working with the currents has left behind traces of its presence in the great standing stones found in some parts of the world. An upright stone, properly positioned, becomes a channel for the solar current, drawing the current down from the skies and sending it into the earth. Standing stones are balanced by sacred springs and trees, which serve to draw the telluric current up from the depths and send it into the sky, completing the cycle. The balance between standing stone and sacred well was used in the most basic form of the art and has left traces in some old Druid rituals, including one of the rituals in this book.

Over thousands of years, ancient peoples developed that basic form in many different directions. Temples, towers, stone circles, earthen mounds, and many other structures rose to help them direct, store, and use the forces of the two currents. In more recent ages, most of the old lore of the two currents has been forgotten, but researchers are beginning to recover some of the lost secrets. Meanwhile, where standing stones still exist, farmers know that their livestock can usually be found gathered around the old standing stones, drawn there by a force most humans cannot detect, and local folklore dimly recalls the days when something that was done with the stones made the land more fertile than it is today.

CONTACTING THE TWO CURRENTS

While it may be a little difficult for most of us to set up a standing stone or locate a sacred well, the subtle connections between human beings and the two currents make it possible for each of us to make contact with the solar and telluric currents ourselves. The two exercises that follow are among the simplest ways to do this. Like many spiritual exercises, they use breathing and imagination to link the mind with the subtle realms of existence that surround us at every moment. Each of these practices should be done at least once while you are preparing for your Druid initiation; you can do them more often if you like. Many Druids, in fact, do practices of this kind every day, for the more often you do them, the more vivid, powerful, and effective they become.

To contact the solar current, stand or sit upright with your feet apart and your spine comfortably straight. If you are outdoors and the sun is up, be aware of it; if not, imagine the sun high above you, streaming down golden light on you and everything around you. Spend a few moments being aware of the sun. While you do this, breathe slowly and gently. Then imagine the sun's light streaming into your body through the crown of your head, lighting up your head with its golden light. Imagine the light flowing downward into your neck, your shoulders, your chest and arms, and so on, all the way through your body, until every part of you is full of golden sunlight. Hold that image in your imagination for a little while, and then gently release it. Don't imagine the light leaving you—let it remain with you, energizing and blessing you as you go about your day.

To contact the telluric current, stand or sit in the same position, with your feet flat on the ground or the floor. If you are outdoors and your feet are resting on grass or soil or stone, be aware of the earth beneath you; if you are indoors or your feet are on an artificial surface, imagine that they are resting on grass. Spend a few moments being aware of the earth beneath you. While you do this, breathe slowly and gently. Then imagine a silvery light, like water from a spring, bubbling up through the soles of your feet, filling your feet with cool, silvery energy. Imagine the energy rising up through your legs, your hips and buttocks, your belly, and so on, all the way to the top of your head, until every part of you is full of the energy. Hold that image in your imagination for a little while and then gently release it. Don't imagine the light leaving you; as with the solar current, let the telluric current remain with you, calming and blessing you as you go about your day.

Contacting the solar current is easiest when you are outdoors in the daytime with nothing but sky and outside space between you and the sun. Contacting the telluric current, in turn, is easiest when you are standing barefoot on the earth with nothing but grass and soil and stone between you and the heart of the earth. It is possible to do both these exercises in other situations, however, and you will find with practice that when you are indoors, shut away temporarily from the world of nature, you can perform either or both of these practices and reconnect yourself with the two currents and the living earth. Try it and see how it changes your state of consciousness.

CHAPTER 6

The Three Rays

THE SYMBOL OF THE THREE RAYS OF LIGHT
—/|\— is the emblem of Druidry and the symbol of
the Druid Revival tradition. This emblem fills much
the same role in Druidry that the yin-yang symbol fills
in Taoism or the cross in Christianity. You will see the
three rays in the seals and emblems of many Druid organizations, and they are carved on monuments and tomb-
stones in Wales and elsewhere. According to Druid
legend, it was by these three rays of light that the world
was created in the beginning of time. The left-hand
ray is called the ray of knowledge, the right-hand ray is
called the ray of power, and the central ray is called the
ray of peace.

The symbol of the three rays has an important lesson
to teach. The two angled rays on the sides of the symbol,
the rays of knowledge and power, represent every pair of
opposites in the world. The human mind naturally thinks

of things in terms of opposites—light and darkness, day and night, matter and energy, life and death, and so on. That's a useful habit in some ways, but it can also become a source of many mistakes and misunderstandings. Once you look at a situation purely in terms of opposites, after all, it can be easy not to notice that most things don't actually belong to either side of the opposition, and that the two extremes very often have more in common with each other than they do with the states or conditions between them.

Take the opposites light and darkness. If you look around yourself, you'll quickly notice that almost everything you see falls between blinding light and total darkness. Even the things that are well lit have shadows, and even the things that are in shadow have some light present. Light and darkness are the two extreme ends of visual experience, and they have something in common that isn't shared by the states between them: you can't see clearly in blinding light, any more than you can in total darkness.

These pairs of opposites are called binaries. According to Druid philosophy, the way to deal with a binary so that it doesn't mislead you is to turn it into a ternary. You do this by finding a third factor that falls in between the two ends of the binary: the middle ray of peace between the two extremes of knowledge without power and power without knowledge. Between light and darkness, for example, the third factor is color: colors are neither pure light nor pure darkness but fall between the two extremes. In the same way, the binary of day and night becomes a ternary when you think about twilight, and so on through the binaries of the world.

This may seem like a pointless exercise, but it becomes a valuable tool when you apply it to the conflicts that shape so many of our lives. Very often we tend to think of such conflicts in terms of two and only two options. Find a third option between the two extremes, and very often this breaks down the opposition between them and allows you to find a solution to the conflict. This is called converting a binary into a ternary. As generations of Druids have found out, too, once you can find a third option, it's usually much easier to find a fourth, a fifth, and so on out to infinity.

Try this for yourself. The next time you see a news story about a conflict of any kind, read the story and think about the two sides of the conflict. What does each side want? What do they fear? What are they trying to achieve? How do they resemble each other? Once you have a clear sense of the two ends of the binary, imagine a third side—a viewpoint different from either of the two in the story, which has its own list of things it wants to achieve or avoid. See what it does to your understanding of the conflict to change it from a binary to a ternary.

THE THREE RAYS OF LIGHT

The three rays also have a central part in a legend that first appears in the bardic writings of Iolo Morganwg—a story set at the beginning of the world, full of symbols and secrets. There are several different versions of the story. One of them runs like this:

> In the beginning of time, Einigan the Giant, the first of all
> created beings, saw three rays of light descending from the
> heavens, which had in them all the knowledge that ever was or
> ever will be. He took three staves of rowan wood and carved on

the branches the forms of signs of all knowledge so that none of it would be forgotten. In time, however, those who saw the rowan staves misunderstood, and worshiped them as gods instead of learning from the knowledge written on them. When he saw this, Einigan was greatly distressed. So great was his grief that he burst into pieces, and after his death the rowan staves were lost.

When a year and a day had passed since the death of Einigan, Menw son of Teirwaedd happened across the skull of Einigan and found that the three rowan staves had taken root and were growing out of the mouth of the skull. He found that by careful study he was able to read some of the writing on the staves. From the lore that he learned, Menw became the first of the gwyddons, the loremasters of the Celts in the most ancient times, before the Druids, and it was from the gwyddons that the secrets of the three rays of light were passed down to the Druids who came after them.

This legend has long had an important role in Druid teaching, and one of the reasons for its importance is what it has to say about legends themselves. Like the three rowan staves, legends are meant to be studied and understood, not worshiped; the important thing about them is not whether they happened, but what they mean. In a literal sense, Einigan, Menw, and the three rowan staves never existed, but their meanings are all around us at every moment.

We can explore one set of those meanings here. Einigan is the soul, the innermost spark of every human being, which is the only part of us that can experience spiritual realities directly. The three rays of light are those spiritual realities, and the three rowan staves stand for all the attempts that have been made by saints, sages, and visionaries down through the ages to communicate what they have experienced to people who have not yet had personal contact with spiritual realities. Too often, people mistake these forms and symbols for the living spiritual experiences they are meant to communicate, and when that happens, the potential for awakening wisdom can easily be lost.

Menw, the mind, is the power in each of us that can recover the lost secrets. The mind is not the soul, and it does not have the ability to experience spiritual realities itself, but it can understand the forms and symbols that reflect spiritual realities. Think of the way that someone familiar with the outdoors can see marks in the soil or snow and know that a deer made them as it walked through the forest the evening before. In the same way, your mind can find and follow the tracks of spiritual realities and lead you to the point at which your soul can begin to perceive those realities directly. The practices of Druidry, which are covered in the next section of this book, are meant to help you train your mind in this way.

CHAPTER 7

The
Four
Elements

IN ANCIENT TIMES, PEOPLE DID NOT YET HAVE
the tools of modern science, but they had keen senses
and paid close attention to the world in which they lived.
Like everyone in every age, they came up with categories to help them sort out the world. Four of the most
important of these categories were the most general
kinds of "stuff" they found around them, which they
called the four elements: Earth, Water, Air, and Fire.
(These words are capitalized to make it clear that the
elements are not the same as the material substances
that gave them their names.)

Nowadays the word "element" is used for the basic
atomic substances of matter, but the same four categories are still used under other names. What the
ancients called the element of Earth, scientists today
call solid matter. The things the ancients assigned to
the element of Water are now called liquids, and the

things the ancients put in the category of Air are now called gases. The element of Fire? These days it's called energy. Whether you call them solids, liquids, gases, and energy, or Earth, Water, Fire, and Air, these four categories make it easier to make sense of the world.

The ancient teaching of the four elements has an important place in Druidry and in many other spiritual traditions, because the four elements are not just categories of matter and energy—they are also symbols. Even today we can talk of an earthy joke or a fiery temper; we have all met the sort of person who can be described as an airhead, and many of us can still remember the days when someone who was clueless could be described as "all wet." The four elements thus make tools to think with. Once we learn how to use them as tools, we can use them to help us understand the world around us, and also to understand ourselves.

For example, think about the ways you experience the world and yourself. You have the inputs from your ordinary senses; you have your feelings; you have your thoughts; and you have the subtle senses that, in most people, are experienced as intuition: the sudden flash of wordless knowledge or "gut feeling" that comes from the realm of the spirit. Those four functions of consciousness correspond to the four elements—sensations to Earth, feelings to Water, thoughts to Air, and intuitions to Fire. The famous psychologist Carl Jung noticed that nearly everyone has one of these ways of knowing about the world as what he called the "dominant function," the source of information on which they habitually rely. Which of these is your dominant function?

EARTH

WATER

AIR

FIRE

In the traditional lore of the elements, the four elements are placed in the diagram above, with Fire opposite Earth and Air opposite Water. One of the lessons of this diagram is that it helps you find one of your own weak spots. Jung and other psychologists have found that the opposite of your dominant function is usually your weakest function. Very often, people who rely on their ability to think have trouble feeling clearly, and in the same way, people who rely on their emotions very often have trouble thinking clearly. In the same way, down-to-earth people who pay attention to what their five senses tell them very often ignore their own intuition, while strongly intuitive people don't usually pay enough attention to what their senses are telling them. Once you know what your dominant function is, see if you can learn to pay more attention to the opposite function. You'll find that this helps you notice many things you would have missed and avoid certain troubles that might otherwise have happened to you.

The elements are also associated in Druid tradition with the four directions. East is assigned to Air, south to Fire, west to Water, and north to Earth. It's important not to take these symbolic connections too literally, since of course there are solids, liquids, gases, and energy in all four of these directions. Furthermore, depending on where you live, the sea may be north, east, or south of you instead of west, and so on. The assignment of elements to directions is mostly a convenience in ritual. As you'll see, it helps to be able to give each element its own location in ritual space.

The exercises that follow can help you understand and develop a feeling for each of the four elements. Each of them should be done at least once while you are preparing for your Druid initiation, and you can do them more often—one each week, repeating the sequence over and over again, would not be too much. Do them in the order in which they appear on pages 73–77: Earth, then Water, then Air, and finally Fire.

CONTACTING THE EARTH ELEMENT

To contact the element of Earth you will need to find a place where you can sit directly on the ground. The surface you sit on doesn't have to be bare soil—it can be a spot covered with grass, for example, and it also works to do this exercise sitting on a natural boulder or a rock surface—but nothing artificial should be between you and the ground. Sit down and place your hands so your fingertips are touching the ground. Let yourself relax and pay attention to your surroundings. Take three deep, slow breaths to begin the exercise.

Then imagine that you are sinking gently into the ground. Feel the soil all around you. If there are plants in the place where you are sitting, be aware of their roots reaching down into the soil. Imagine yourself sinking farther, and farther still, until you have reached rock. Feel the earth around you: heat rising up from the molten realms of the mantle far below you, the stone around you, and the layers of soil above you, finishing with the topsoil on which your body is sitting. Make the experience as vivid as you can. After a few minutes, imagine yourself rising slowly back up to the surface.

Once you have returned to your body, draw in a deep breath, and as you do, imagine the subtle influences of Earth rising up and filling your body.

Feel yourself take on the strength and stability of the element of Earth. As you breathe out, let the influences of Earth flow out of you, but the strength and stability remain behind. Repeat this until you have drawn in and let out seven deep breaths, each time filling yourself with the strength and stability of Earth. Then let your breathing return to normal. After a little while, when you feel ready, stand up and go on with the rest of your day.

CONTACTING THE WATER ELEMENT

To contact the element of Water you will need to find a place where you can sit near a stream, a river, a lake, or the sea. (If you live in a place far from any of these, travel may be needed.) The closer you can get to the water, the better, but you don't have to be near enough to touch the water—a park bench overlooking a river, or dry sand or driftwood on an ocean beach is fine. Sit down facing the water. Let yourself relax and pay attention to your surroundings. Take three deep, slow breaths to begin the exercise.

Then imagine your consciousness plunging into the water. Feel water flowing and surging around you. Sense the earth beneath the water and the air above the water, and let yourself move with the currents and waves of the water as they dance between these two realms. Be aware that every drop of water that surrounds you, at various times in the past, has been drawn up into the air by evaporation, to fall as rain or snow in some distant place; be aware also that every drop of water that surrounds you, at other times in the past, has been drawn down into the deep places of the earth as groundwater, to rise up again to the surface in a spring or well. Make the experience as vivid as you can. After a few minutes, imagine yourself returning to your body on the shore.

Once you have returned to your body, draw in a deep breath, and as you do, imagine the subtle influences of Water flowing toward you and filling your body. Feel yourself take on the strength and flowing grace of the element of Water. As you breathe out, let the influences of Water flow out of you, but the strength and grace remain behind. Repeat this until you have drawn in and let out seven deep breaths, each time filling yourself with the strength and grace of Water. Then let your breathing return to normal. After a little while, when you feel ready, stand up and go on with the rest of your day.

CONTACTING THE AIR ELEMENT

To contact the element of Air you will need to find a place where you can sit beneath the open sky. This exercise is best done on a high place, such as a hill or ridge, or on a balcony or the roof of a building. Sit down and pay attention to the air around you. Let yourself relax and pay attention to your surroundings. Take three deep, slow breaths to begin the exercise.

Then imagine that you are rising up into the air, floating free like a balloon. Feel the air rushing and flowing around you. Let yourself be aware of the ground beneath you and the sun high above. If there are clouds, watch them drifting past on the wind. Feel the air growing thin and cold as it rises up into the high reaches of the atmosphere, and feel it becoming warm and dense as it descends toward the ground. Make the experience as vivid as you can. After a few minutes, imagine yourself sinking slowly back down to the ground.

Once you have returned to your body, draw in a deep breath, and as you do, imagine the subtle influences of Air rushing toward you and filling your body. Feel yourself take on the strength and agility of the element of Air. As you breathe out, let the influences of Air flow out of you, but the strength and agility remain behind. Repeat this until you have drawn in and let out seven deep breaths, each time filling yourself with the strength and agility of Air. Then let your breathing return to normal. After a little while, when you feel ready, stand up and go on with the rest of your day.

CONTACTING THE FIRE ELEMENT

To contact the element of Fire you have two choices. You can find a place where you can light a fire safely—a candle flame will do, though if you have access to a fireplace or a fire pit where you can build a campfire, it will often result in a more vivid and powerful experience. Alternatively, you can find a place where you can sit facing the sun, the heart of the element of Fire in the world of nature. Light the candle or the fire, or turn toward the sun, and sit down facing the flames. Let yourself relax and pay attention to your surroundings. Take three deep, slow breaths to begin the exercise.

Then imagine your consciousness plunging into the heart of the flame. Feel the heat and light streaming outward through you. Sense what surrounds the flame, whether it is the cool air around a candle flame or the tremendous cold and silence of outer space surrounding the mighty flame of the sun. Make the experience as vivid as you can. After a few minutes, imagine your consciousness returning to your body.

Once you have returned to your body, draw in a deep breath, and as you do, imagine the subtle influences of Fire shining on you and filling your body. Feel yourself take on the strength and brilliance of the element of Fire. As you breathe out, let the influences of Fire flow out of you, but the strength
and brilliance remain behind. Repeat this
until you have drawn in and let out seven
deep breaths, each time filling yourself with the strength and brilliance of
Fire. Then let your breathing return to
normal. After a little while, when you
feel ready, stand up and go on with the
rest of your day.

PART THREE

THE
PRACTICE
OF
DRUIDRY

A S WE HAVE SEEN ALREADY, BEING A DRUID IS not a matter of accepting this or that belief or belonging to this or that organization. More generally, Druidry is not something you are, it's something you do. This is why most Druids these days like to call the path they follow Druidry rather than Druidism. Think of other words that end in "-ism," and you'll find that most of them are ideologies—that is to say, collections of opinions and beliefs.

Druidry is not an ideology. Like basketry, forestry, and many other words that end with -ry, it can best be understood as a craft. You don't become a basket maker or a forester by believing some set of opinions. You become a basket maker by learning and practicing basketry, and you become a forester by learning and practicing forestry. In the same way, you become a Druid by learning and practicing the craft of Druidry. One of the things this means is that becoming a Druid isn't an all-or-nothing matter. You start becoming a Druid as soon as you begin learning some elements of the Druid craft, and you keep on becoming a Druid as long as you keep studying and practicing that craft. If you stop studying and practicing, you stop becoming a Druid, and if you don't take up the studies and the practices again, you may lose touch with what you've learned as a Druid, just as a basket maker can lose her skills if she neglects them long enough.

In the approach to Druidry taught in this book, four essential practices make up the craft of the Druid. The practice of observation involves paying close attention to nature. The practice of meditation involves calm, focused, directed thinking about the symbols, teachings, and traditions of Druidry. The practice of divination involves using a set of traditional symbols to awaken the intuition and give you glimpses of present and future patterns taking shape in the One Life. The practice of ritual, finally, involves symbolic actions meant to focus and direct your mind, so that you can transform your relationship with yourself, with nature, and with the One Life that moves through both.

The first three of these practices are receptive. In a very real sense, they are ways of listening—listening to nature, listening to tradition, and listening to intuition. The fourth practice is active, and it can be seen as a way of speaking. Most human beings talk too much and listen too little, so this arrangement of practices is a good reminder that it's wise to listen three times as much as you talk!

One final point to keep in mind before we proceed is that Druids practice their craft in different ways. If you read other books on Druidry, meet other Druids, or interact with Druid organizations, you will find that many of them have their own unique ways of practicing meditation, divination, and ritual that differ from the ones given in this book. (Nature observation is a little less variable, as sitting quietly with your eyes and ears wide open is pretty much the only option there is.) The specific techniques given in this book are simply one set of practices. You always have the option, as you learn other ways of practicing the craft of Druidry, to try unfamiliar ways of doing things and to explore the possibility that some of those ways may be included in the work you do as you follow the Druid path.

PRACTICING DRUIDRY WITH OTHERS

Druidry can be a solitary path, but it does not have to be. Many Druids like to work with others at least some of the time. This book is designed for the solitary practitioner, but it can also be used by a group of friends who

want to walk the Druid path together. The most important point to keep in mind, if you decide to do this, is that working with others is not a substitute for following the Druid path yourself.

If you are working with a group, for example, you can do sessions of observation together: going someplace where there are plenty of trees and other living things, sitting quietly together, and signaling with a silent gesture and a pointed finger when something comes into view.

Group meditation is also well worth doing—when the members of a group choose a theme together, meditate on it together in silence, and when everyone is finished, discuss what they have learned about it, everyone can learn more about the theme than they would have done in solitary meditation. Casting and interpreting divinations for other people is a very good way to develop your skills as a diviner, and it can also be very useful for one person to cast a reading and all the members of the group to discuss what it means and how it relates to the situation it was cast to explore.

Finally, group rituals can be powerful experiences, and a group of people who learn how to work together can make each ritual a beautiful and moving experience.

None of these things, however, should be a replacement for your own solitary Druid practice. It's by working alone that you will develop the skills in observation, meditation, divination, and ritual that will enable you to work well with others. Above all, the preparations for your initiation, and the initiation ritual itself, should be strictly private. Those are to be done by yourself, for yourself.

What if you can't find anyone else interested in following the Druid path with you, or you discover that you don't really get along with the other

people in your area who have taken up Druidry, or if you simply don't want to work with a group and would rather pursue Druidry as a solitary practice? That's fine too. The heart of Druidry is your relationship to the world of nature and the spiritual powers that express themselves in nature. Working with other human beings comes second to that, and if for whatever reason that's not a workable option for you, the Druid path is still open to you.

CHAPTER 8

Observation

DRUIDRY IS A WAY OF NATURE SPIRITUALITY—
that is, a spiritual path that focuses on your relationship
to the natural world. One of the things that this implies
is that observing nature is one of the basic spiritual practices for Druids. To watch atttentively as the patterns of
nature unfold, to learn from those patterns, and to apply
the lessons the patterns teach to your own life and to
your understanding of the world: these will be essential
steps in your journey toward wisdom as a Druid.

Too many people think of nature as something
that only exists off in the distance, in exotic environments supposedly undisturbed by human activities.
This mistaken notion is one of the hidden sources of
the environmental problems of our time, because people
who fall into that habit of thought too often lose track of
the importance of the natural patterns and processes all
around them, on which their own lives depend. Once you

become attentive to nature all around you, by contrast, it becomes easier to notice what parts of your lifestyle are contributing to the environmental problems of our time—and to see the simple and gentle steps you can take to make your lifestyle part of the solution instead.

Nature is everywhere. If you look at the sky and watch the clouds drift past or see rain or snow fall, you witness nature at work. If you notice where weeds grow through cracks in the concrete, see which plants attract bees and butterflies, hear the scuttling in the undergrowth that tells you

that some living creature is going about its life there, you are taking an important step on the Druid path. It can be a magical experience to travel to some spot of great natural beauty far away, of course, but you can have experiences just as magical right where you live, by opening your eyes and your other senses to find out what nature is doing there.

You can begin the journey by finding a place where you can sit among plants and see the sky. It can be as simple as a corner of your backyard, a local park, or even an apartment balcony or an open window with a window box full of herbs outside it and a good view of the sky in one direction. It can be something more than this if you have the opportunity, but starting the practice is more important than getting everything just the way you want it. Nature writer Ernest Thompson Seton used to repeat a fine maxim that many Druids nowadays keep in mind: "Where you are, with what you have, right now."

Once you have your place, what do you do? Just sit still and observe. Most people these days never take the time to stop and watch what nature is doing. As a Druid, you know better. Calmly, attentively, watch the sky, the plants, and anything else natural that you can see. Notice the sounds that come to your ears and the smells that reach you with each breath. Open your senses and pay attention. The more often you do this, the easier it will become, the more you will notice, and the clearer and more observant your senses and your mind will become.

By the way, this isn't a time to read, listen to music, text your friends, play video games, or do anything else besides paying attention to nature. It's also not a time to think. If you catch your mind chattering at you or notice that you're getting caught up in your feelings about something unrelated to what's around you right there and then, set your thoughts and feelings aside and return to observing. Whatever the distraction is, you can go back to thinking and feeling about it later, once you've finished your practice.

Spend time this way at least once a week. Start with five minutes of still, silent attention to nature, and increase that once five minutes are easy. When you have made your weekly session of observation a regular habit, see if it's convenient for you to fit a second session each week into your schedule. Some Druids make a point of going outside first thing in the morning every day and spending five or ten minutes paying attention to nature before starting their other activities, but only you can decide if this works for you.

NATURE STUDY

You can enrich your observation practice by learning something about nature in the area where you live. It's one thing to notice a big white bird of an unfamiliar kind perched in a tree not far from where you are sitting and quite another to know enough about the local birds to realize that a snowy owl has come winging its way south from its usual haunts in the Arctic to pay a visit to your neighborhood! Equally, when you know the names and life cycles of the trees where you live, they stop being green blobs and turn into individuals, young or old, healthy or ill, living their own lives in company with yours.

It's fairly easy nowadays in most parts of the world to find books that will tell you how to identify the birds, trees, and plants that live where you do. It can take a little more work to find books that will teach you how to identify the animals that live in your area, but the effort is worth making. This is true even if you live in a city. Tracker and nature educator Tom Brown Jr., in his classic book *Tom Brown's Field Guide to the Forgotten Wilderness* (1987), describes watching a wild weasel hunting mice in a parking lot on the Lower East Side of Manhattan, one of the most ferociously urbanized places in North America. Many other people who have learned to pay attention to nature have had similar experiences.

In urban Rhode Island, where I live, I've watched rabbits, raccoons, skunks, and foxes going about their lives, to say nothing of the ubiquitous gray squirrels and field mice common in most urban areas. Above the ground, aside from familiar birds such as sparrows and robins, I've watched northern goshawks, kestrels, merlins, harriers, and now and then a bald eagle. Once, I caught sight of a glorious iron-gray gyrfalcon that must have flown down this way from Greenland, where they usually live. Great blue herons are common here, sweeping through the sky with slow, patient wingbeats. At night, I've watched bats of two different species swooping

and darting as they fill up on tasty mosquitoes and moths. Wherever you live, whether it's in a city, a suburb, a small town, or in the country, there are wild things living nearby. If you get to know them and learn about their lives, this will help you attune yourself to the cycles of nature around you.

While you're doing this, you might also learn something about the land on which you live. In many places you can find books of local geology intended for people who aren't geologists, and these are well worth reading as part of your Druid studies. To me, it adds a certain perspective—and a certain magic!—to know that fifteen thousand years ago, during the last Ice Age, the place where I live had a layer of glacial ice half a mile thick on top of it, and that five hundred million years ago, the rocks beneath my feet were part of a small continent that geologists call Avalonia, which broke apart when dinosaurs walked the earth, and now makes up parts of New England, Canada's Maritime Provinces, southern Ireland, Wales, and England.

The ancient Druids paid close attention to the cycles of nature. They watched the clouds and winds, followed the courses of the streams, studied plants and stones, noticed the birds and animals around them. The attunement with nature that followed from these studies helped give them their reputation for great wisdom. From the dawn of the Druid Revival until the present, modern Druids have done the same things and achieved the same attunement with nature. Making the observation and study of nature part of your own Druid path will help you to follow in their footsteps.

RESOURCES FOR OBSERVATION

Most of the things you need in order to practice observing are your own body and mind and a place where you can sit and watch the natural world. A few books to help you learn the local birds, animals, trees, and plants can also be helpful, and if you find birds especially interesting, a pair of binoculars can help you figure out exactly what just came flying out of the distance to perch in the oak across the street. As a general rule, though, anything that distracts you from direct, personal experience of things in nature is an obstacle rather than a help, so leave telephoto lenses, guidebooks, and the rest of the kit behind when you go out to spend a few minutes observing nature.

Two things you may find useful to bring along, by contrast, are a pen and a small notebook that can fit in a pocket. It will often happen that you spot a bird, a plant, an animal, or some other thing in nature that you don't recognize. If you take a moment to write down a quick description or make a little sketch, you can use that after you've finished your period of observation and return home to look up in a guidebook what you saw. Some Druids like to take this further and keep a nature journal, in which they record each day what is happening in the natural world around them. If this interests you, by all means explore it.

Depending on where you live, you may be able to find classes on local birds, wildlife, and the like, or organizations devoted to preserving and enjoying local natural places. These can be useful if they give you information about the local environment or opportunities to visit places with well-informed guides, but they can also be a hindrance rather than a help if too much of their focus is on human activities rather than the world of nature. Explore the options if you find you're inter- ested in doing so, but remember that there is no replacement for time spent sitting quietly with your senses open and your mouth shut, paying attention to what nature is doing.

CHAPTER 9

Meditation

THE SAME QUALITY OF CALM, FOCUSED ATTEN-
tion that is central to the practice of observation also plays
an important role in the second core practice of modern
Druidry, which is meditation. The kind of meditation
most Druids practice is a little different, and noticeably
easier for most people, than the Asian forms of meditation that have become so popular in the Western world
in recent years. In the same way that observation teaches
you to use your senses, Druid meditation teaches you to
use your mind. Your goal in this stage of the work is not
to stifle your thoughts but to learn how to direct them,
attend to them, and use them as a tool for making sense
of the symbols and stories of the ancient Celts and the
Druid Revival tradition.

Too many people these days think of meditation
as something mysterious and exotic and have no idea
that the Western world has any meditation systems

of its own. Just a century and a half ago, when the Druid Revival was in full flower, most people knew better. Many churches taught it to their congregations, and there were plenty of books in print explaining how to meditate and setting out subjects for meditation. Fortunately, the Western way of meditation is being recovered now, and Druids are among those who are making that happen.

There's nothing particularly strange or exotic about the kind of meditation we're discussing. It's simply what happens when you focus your mind on one subject and keep it there, instead of letting it jump from one topic to another at random, the way it usually does. The English word "meditation," in fact, comes from a Latin word meaning "thinking." Think for a moment about the word "premeditated," which is used in criminal law. When you say that a crime was premeditated, you don't mean that the person responsible sat in lotus posture and chanted a mantra before committing the crime! You mean that the criminal thought through what he was going to do before he did it.

Meditation, in other words, is calm, focused, directed thinking. Generations of practice and experience have shown that if this sort of thinking is combined with certain simple habits of posture and breathing, and directed toward certain traditional symbols and stories, the result is an effective means of spiritual development that can be practiced by anyone without the supervision of a teacher. That was why meditation was so common a century and a half ago, and it is one half of the reason why the Druids of the Revival took it up so enthusiastically from the eighteenth century onward.

The other half of the reason is that something very close to this kind of meditation may have been practiced by the ancient Druids, and was certainly practiced by the Irish, Scottish, and Welsh bards who inherited some of the secrets of the ancient Druids. Writings about the Scottish bardic schools, where the old traditions seem to have survived the longest, describe how students used to lie down in solitary rooms, place rocks on their bellies to make them aware of their breathing, and concentrate on the traditional stories and poems they knew or compose poetry of their own. The posture that Druids now use for meditation is different, and there are other ways to learn to pay attention to the rhythms of breath, but the principle is much the same.

One other difference to keep in mind is that ancient Druidry was founded before the Celts knew about writing, and throughout its history Druids were expected to commit the teachings to memory rather than writing them down. The Scottish bards just mentioned lived long after writing had come to Scotland, but in their time paper and ink were very expensive and they still learned poems and stories by heart. Some Druids today do the same thing, but it's very common for Druid meditation to use themes—subjects for calm, focused, directed thinking—taken out of books on Druidry or on the myths and legends of Celtic peoples. How this is done will be explained a little later in this section.

PRELIMINARIES FOR MEDITATION

For all of the meditation exercises in this chapter, you'll need a place that is quiet and not too brightly lit. It should be private—a room with a door you can shut is best, though if you can't arrange that, a quiet corner, and a little forbearance on the part of your housemates will do the job. You'll need a chair with a straight back, and a seat at a height that allows you to rest your feet flat on the floor while keeping your thighs parallel with the ground. You'll need a clock or watch, placed so that you can see it easily without moving your head.

How often you practice meditation is something only you can decide. Many Druids find that practicing meditation every day brings the best results, and some organizations recommend that their members meditate first thing each morning, but you may or may not be able to make time for this in your schedule. If once a week is what works for you, then make that the rhythm of your practice. You may find, though, that meditation's power to calm and center your mind is welcome enough that you change your schedule to make room for it.

The posture to use for your Druid meditations is much simpler and, for most people, more comfortable, than the half-lotus and full lotus postures used in Asian methods of meditation. Sit on your chair with your feet flat on the floor and your legs fairly close together—they don't have to be touching but it's usually best for them to be parallel. Your back should be upright but not stiff, and your

chin tucked in just a little, so you feel a slight stretch at the back of your neck. Your eyes may be open or closed as you prefer. If they're open, they should look ahead of you but not focus on anything in particular. Once you've gotten settled into the posture, you can proceed to the first of the preliminary exercises.

The key to meditation is learning to enter a state of relaxed concentration. The word "relaxed" needs to be kept in mind here. Too many people today, when they hear the word "concentration," think of a kind of inner struggle in which the body is tensed, the eyes narrowed, the teeth gritted, and so on. This is the opposite of the state you need to reach. The exercises below will help you get to that state of calm focus that will allow meditation to happen.

Preliminary Exercise I

To begin learning how to meditate, put yourself in the meditation position, and then spend five minutes by the clock just being aware of your physical body. Start at the soles of your feet, your contact points with the earth and the telluric current, and shift your attention slowly upward from there, a little at a time, to the crown of your head, your contact point with the sky and the solar current. Take your time and notice any tensions you feel. Don't try to make yourself relax; simply be aware of any tension you notice. Over time this simple act of awareness will dissolve your body's tensions by making them conscious, and it will also gradually bring up the rigid patterns of thought and emotion that underlie your tensions. Like so much in meditation, though, this process has to unfold at its own pace.

While you're doing this exercise, keep your body as still as possible. You will very likely feel a temptation to fidget and shift. Don't give into it. Whenever your body starts itching, cramping, or feeling uncomfortable, simply be aware of that, without doing anything about it. These reactions often become very intrusive during the first month or so of meditation practice, but bear with them. They show you that you're getting past the shallow state of ordinary awareness in which most people spend most of their time. All these discomforts have been in your body all along; you've simply learned not to notice them. Now that you can perceive them again, you can relax into them and let them go.

Preliminary Exercise 2

Do the first preliminary exercise five or six times, each time on a different day, until the posture starts to feel comfortable and balanced. After that, it's time to bring in the next element of meditation, which is breathing. Start by settling your meditation position and going through the first exercise quickly, passing your awareness through your body from the soles of your feet to the top of your head, as a way of "checking in" with your physical body and settling into a comfortable and stable position. Then turn your attention to your breath. Draw in a deep breath, and expel it slowly and steadily, until your lungs are completely empty.

When every last puff of air is out of your lungs, hold the breath out while counting slowly and steadily from one to four. Then breathe in through your nose, smoothly and evenly, counting from one to four, and imagining a current of the One Life flowing into you, bringing in life and wisdom. Hold your breath in, counting from one to four; it's important to hold the breath in by keeping the chest and belly expanded, not by forcing your throat shut, which can hurt your lungs. (If you can breathe in a little more while holding your breath, without hearing or feeling a "pop" from inside your throat, you're doing it right.) Then breathe out through your nose, smoothly and evenly, again counting from one to four, and imagining a current of the One Life flowing out of you, taking all tensions and distractions with it. Finally, keep your lungs empty, again counting from one to four. Continue breathing in this same slow steady rhythm, counting in the same way, for five minutes by the clock. This pattern of breathing is called the Fourfold Breath, and it's traditional in the Western method of meditation.

While you're breathing, your thoughts will likely try to wander away to something other than the exercise that you're doing. When this happens, bring your attention back to the rhythm of the breathing, the feeling of the air moving into and out of your lungs, and the sense of the One Life flowing into you and out from you. You'll probably need to bring your attention back to your breathing over and over again, especially in the first few months you spend practicing meditation. Over time, you'll find it easier to keep your mind centered on the simple process of breathing.

As that happens, the first benefits of meditation may begin to show themselves. Most people find that they become calmer and more focused after a session of meditation, even if all that's involved is this kind of steady rhythmic breathing. You may also find that your body is less tense, and some people even find that they need less sleep when they meditate every day.

PRACTICING MEDITATION

Do the second preliminary exercise five or six times, until the Fourfold Breath feels familiar, easy and comfortable to you. At this point it's time to bring in the third dimension of meditation practice, the dimension of the mind. Once you have done that, you have finished the preliminaries and have started on the adventure of meditation itself.

In order to practice meditation, you need a *theme*. This is the subject of your meditation, the concept, symbol, or sentence of a text you want to understand better. Druid meditation, remember, is calm, focused, directed thinking, so you need something to think about!

You can use anything that interests you as a source of themes for meditation. For many Druids, especially Pagan Druids, the old Celtic myths and legends are a traditional and reliable source of themes. Christian Druids very often supplement these with verses drawn from the Bible. Books on Druid philosophy and Celtic tradition are another popular source. There are many others, and some specific suggestions will be made a little later in this section.

As you get ready for your initiation as a Druid, you'll be asked to meditate on the One Life, the two currents, the three rays of light, and the four elements. Doing this will give you an idea of how to extract themes from a text. The key to the entire process is to look for things that make you ask yourself "what does this mean?" Meditation is how you answer that question.

Two hints will help you get the most out of each theme. The first is to take big ideas in small bites. Rather than trying to grasp an entire text, concept, or symbolic image in a single session of meditation, start with one

small part of it, devote an entire session of meditation to that, and then go on to another part in the next session. If you're exploring a Celtic legend using meditation, for example, don't try to make sense of the whole legend at once. Take it one character or event at a time and see what that has to say to you before going on.

The second hint is to let yourself meditate on the same theme repeatedly, for as long as you keep getting new ideas to explore. The meditations you will be asked to do on the One Life, the two currents, the three rays of light, and the four elements, for example, will get you started making sense of them—but those meditations are only a start. Take your time, repeat each theme until you run out of new ideas to explore, and remember that there are no prizes for hurrying. One theme that you have unpacked thoroughly in many sessions of meditation will teach you more and take you farther than a hundred you have barely skimmed.

Once you have chosen your theme, you are ready to meditate. Sit down in the meditation posture and spend a minute or two going through the first preliminary exercise, being aware of your body and its tensions. Then begin the fourfold breath and continue it for five minutes by the clock. During these first steps, don't think about the theme, or for that matter anything else. Simply be aware, first of your body and its tensions, then of the rhythm and pattern of your breathing, and allow your mind to become clear.

After five minutes, change from the fourfold breath to ordinary, slow breathing. At this point bring your theme to mind. Consider it for a little while, as though it were a stone you found in the forest, and you were turning it over to see every side of it. Think about it in a general way. Then choose one of the thoughts that come to mind, and follow it out step by step, thinking about its meaning and implications, taking it as far as you can. There are no right or wrong answers in meditation, so don't worry about whether you're "getting it right." Just see what your thoughts have to say about the theme. Once you're ready to end the meditation, draw in a deep breath, let it out slowly and smoothly, and then get up and go on with the rest of your day.

An example may help make sense of this process. Let's say you're meditating on the One Life, the first teaching covered in chapter 4 and the first theme for the meditations you will do to prepare for your initiation as a Druid. After the preliminaries, you turn your mind toward the idea of the One Life and think about it in a general way. What does it mean to suggest that all living things share one life? That this same life is also present, though less obvious, in things our culture labels as "not alive"? That life is a force that flows through all things, more visible in some, less visible in others? That your life, from your conception and birth right up to the present moment, is part of that flowing life? Questions like these, as they come to mind, will help you explore the theme and understand what it has to teach you.

After you've done this for a time, you choose one idea that came to mind while you were thinking about the One Life and focus on it. Let's say the idea that catches your interest during this session of meditation is the vision of the One Life as more visible and more active in some things than in others. You think about stones, plants, animals, and human beings, each with a different way of expressing the One Life, and you notice that there are transitions between these categories. Crystals, for example, grow like plants; some plants move in response to things around them, like animals; some animals display complex intelligence, like humans. Thinking about this, you become aware of one of the lessons implied in the Druid teaching

of the One Life—the vision of that life flowing slowly but surely through all things, expressing itself in richer and more complex ways over time. You might catch a glimpse of the One Life as a process rather than a thing. In future meditations, you can then take this insight even further.

Unless you have quite a bit of experience in meditation, your thoughts will likely wander away from the theme again and again. Instead of simply bringing them back in a jump, follow them back through the chain of wandering thoughts until you reach the point where they left the theme. If you're meditating on the One Life, for example, and you suddenly notice that you're thinking about your Aunt Alice instead, don't simply go back to the One Life and start again. Work your way back. What got you thinking about Aunt Alice? Memories of a Christmas dinner at her home when you were a child. What called up that memory? Recalling the taste of the roasted mixed nuts she used to put out for the guests. Where did that come from? Thinking about squirrels. Why squirrels? Because you heard the scuttling noise of a squirrel running across the roof above you, and it distracted you from thinking about the One Life.

Whenever your mind strays from the theme, bring it back up the track of wandering thoughts in this same way. This approach has two advantages. First of all, it has much to teach about the way your mind works, the flow of its thoughts and the sort of associative leaps it habitually makes. Second, it develops the habit of returning to the theme, and with practice you'll find that your thoughts run back to the theme of your meditations just as enthusiastically as they run away from it. Time and regular practice will shorten the distance they run, until eventually your mind learns to run straight ahead along the meanings and implications of a theme without veering from it at all.

To begin with, five minutes of meditation following the five minutes of the Fourfold Breath is enough. Increase it to ten minutes once it's easy for you to do five minutes at a sitting. Add another five minutes any time you find that you could use more time. For most people, fifteen to twenty minutes of meditation (plus the five minutes of breathing to begin with) is a good amount, and more than thirty minutes a day is rarely useful.

RESOURCES FOR MEDITATION

The most important resource you will need for meditation is a source of themes. This book will provide you with some themes to get started with, but you will need more material by the time you have finished the preparatory work for your initiation as a Druid and have performed the ritual of self-initiation. As already noted, anything that interests you can be used as a source of themes for meditation. If it makes you think, "I wonder what that means," you know you've got a source of good themes for meditation.

Books about Druid teachings and philosophy are one source many Druids find useful for this purpose, and if you are a religious person, of course, the scriptures and symbols of the faith you follow are another classic source. More challenging, but also more rewarding, are books on Celtic myths and legends. Nowadays few people remember that myths and legends aren't simply colorful stories. Everything that appears in them is also a symbol. It means something—in fact, it usually means more than one thing. It can take repeated meditations on the same story to tease out all the meanings that are hidden in the tale.

If you go questing for these hidden meanings, you'll have to make use of your mind in ways that are unfamiliar to most people these days. Questions such as "what does this remind me of?" and "what else goes through changes like this?" are among the tools that will help you at this work. Don't be afraid to explore entirely personal meanings in your meditations. If a character in a legend encounters an obstacle, what obstacles do you face in your own life? What would happen if you faced those obstacles the same way that the character does? What would you be thinking or feeling if you faced the same situation as the character? These and questions like them can help you get past the surface of the story and begin searching its depths.

The same principles apply equally to a third source of themes for meditation that many Druids use—the world of nature. Writers in earlier times liked to speak of the natural world as the Book of Nature, which the wise could learn to read. It can take a great deal of study and practice to begin making sense of nature as a collection of symbols and metaphors, but your practice of observation will help you get started by giving you a clearer sense of what the natural world is doing. Take it slow; remember that there are no right or wrong answers in meditation; and see what you can find. Also see pages 195–201 for a list of books that may be helpful to you on your journey.

CHAPTER 10

Divination

ALONG WITH OBSERVATION AND MEDITATION, divination is a basic Druid practice. Divination is the art of developing intuition through the use of apparently random symbols. The ancient Druids were famous for being able to foretell the future by watching the flight of birds and reading messages from the wind, clouds, and thunder. Modern Druids do the same thing using other methods. One of them, which will be explained in this chapter, is the Coelbren alphabet, a symbolic alphabet that was either invented or rediscovered—no one knows which—by Iolo Morganwg, the Welsh poet who contributed so much to the Druid Revival.

The Coelbren—pronounced KO-ul-bren—is an alphabet of twenty-four letters. At first glance it looks a little like the runes, the divinatory and magical alphabet of the Norse and Germanic tribes of old Europe. The similarity isn't entirely accidental, because both

the runes and the Coelbren were meant to be carved into wood with a knife rather than written with a pen on paper. The shapes and meanings of the Coelbren are not the same as those of the runes, however, and if you're familiar with the runes you'll have to learn a new set of meanings in order to divine with the Coelbren.

The basic process, however, is much the same. To cast a Coelbren reading you will need to make or buy a set of twenty-four sticks, stones, or cards, each of which has one of the Coelbren letters on it. These can be as simple or as fancy as you want them to be—I have done Coelbren readings using plain note cards with the Coelbren letters written on them with a pen, for example, and I have also done readings with a fine set of Coelbren letters carved into wooden sticks in the traditional fashion. If you use sticks or stones, it's a good idea to put them in a cloth bag, so you can draw one or more of them at random without knowing what it is. If you use cards, you can do the same thing, and then shuffle, cut, and deal one or more cards, the way you would when reading tarot cards. Once you have chosen or dealt your Coelbren letters, you can interpret them following the instructions given later in this chapter and understand the message the reading has for you.

How can a set of symbols chosen at random give you insight into the hidden facts of the present and the secrets of the future? There are two reasons, and both of them are involved whenever you practice divination. The first is that nothing in the world is ever really random. The psychologist Carl Jung proposed that a network of subtle connections, which he called "synchronicities," links together everything in the universe, and shapes everything we call random chance. At every moment, those subtle connections form meaningful patterns, and these patterns are expressed in seemingly random events like the flight of birds or the random choice of a stick from a cloth bag. Learning to read those patterns gives insight into what is happening and what will happen.

To read these patterns requires intuition, one of the least understood powers of the human mind. Most of us have had the experience of suddenly knowing something we could not have known in any normal way. People talk about "having a hunch," "getting a gut sense," or "just knowing"— and fairly often that knowledge turns out to be correct. Intuition, the source of these experiences, is the sense by which we tap into the network of synchronicities. Put another way, it's the way we read the meaningful patterns that move through the One Life. Intuition isn't infallible. Just as your eyes can be tricked by an optical illusion, your intuition can be fooled, and you can also get a correct intuition and then misunderstand it. With practice, however, intuition can become a keen and useful way of perceiving the flow of events in the world—and divination is one of the most effective ways to train and develop the intuition.

Bardic Lots or Letters.
Vowels.

C. ∧ ∧Ι ΙΥ ΙΥ Υ Υ Ο Φ V Ѵ
P. a â e ê i u û y o ô w ŵ
R. 1   2   3   4

Consonants.

C. Ι Ѵ Ƀ Ѡ Ι Ι ſ Ρ ſ ζ Κ Ƴ ζ Ȣ
P. b v m m v p ph mh f c ch ngh g ng
N. bi   mi   pi   fi ci   gi
R. 5   6   7   8 9   10

C. ↑ ℿ Ⱶ Ƈ Ɔ Ɖ ᴎ Ɩ Ⱡ Ⱦ Ⰻ Ⱳ ╰
P. t th nh d dh n nl ll r rh s h hw
N. ti   di   ni li   ri   is
R. 11   12   13 14   15   16

PRACTICING DIVINATION

In order to practice divination with the Coelbren alphabet, as already noted, you will need a set of sticks, stones, or cards marked with the Coelbren letters. You can buy a set if you wish, but it works just as well to make them for yourself. The letters themselves are given along with their meanings on pages 118–41. As you look at them, you will notice that some Coelbren letters are mirror images of others—for example, if you flip the letter *Ci* upside down it becomes the letter *Di*, and if you do the same thing to the letter *Li* it becomes the letter *Si*. For this reason, it's important to mark your sticks, stones, or cards so you know which end is up! A dot underneath each letter is one way to do this; another is to put the letter toward one end of the stick, stone, or card, rather than in the middle.

Once you have your Coelbren set, you can proceed to begin casting and interpreting readings with it. There are many different spreads—that is, ways of setting out the Coelbren letters you draw so that you can interpret them—and you will find, as you get some experience with this way of divination, that most spreads designed for tarot cards or runes can be used just as effectively with the Coelbren. To begin with, however, most people find it best to start with a very simple spread and move on to others only after getting some skill with the divination method they are using.

The spread I recommend for beginners to use is called the Three Rays of Light spread, shown below.

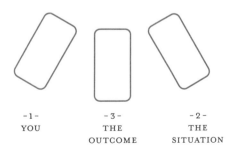

-1-
YOU

-3-
THE
OUTCOME

-2-
THE
SITUATION

The first position, on the left-hand side, represents you or the person for whom you are casting the divination if you are doing a reading for someone else. The second, on the right-hand side, represents the situation you're in, and the third, in the middle, represents the outcome of the situation for you. It's a very simple spread, but you'll find that with practice you can extract plenty of meaning and insight from it. To use it, simply draw three Coelbren sticks, stones, or cards, one at a time, and put them down as shown in the diagram. Then interpret them using the meanings of the three positions. If the first letter you draw is *A*, for example, the basic meaning is that you're doing the right thing and you should keep on doing it. If the second is *Gi*, the basic meaning is that the situation is very complex right now and will change in unpredictable ways in response to your action. If the third is *Li*, the basic meaning is that everything will work out for the best despite these complications.

The most effective way to learn divination is to cast a simple reading like this every day. If you do it in the morning, the question to ask is "what will I encounter this day?" If you do it in the evening, change the question to "what will I encounter tomorrow?" Write the reading down in a notebook and include what you think it is trying to tell you. When the day is over, review the reading and interpretation, and see if you can understand a little more about what the Coelbren was saying to you. As you repeat this process, you'll develop a personal sense of what each of the Coelbren letters means, and this will make it easy to interpret your readings.

THE COELBREN ALPHABET

There are twenty-four letters in the Coelbren alphabet, and each of them represents a condition of movement or change. That's one of the things that makes the Coelbren different from other oracles. The positions in each spread stand for people, things, and events—think of the way that the first position in the Three Rays of Light spread stands for you (a person), the second for your situation (a thing), and the third for the outcome (an event). The Coelbren letter that turns up in each position tells you what will happen to that person, thing, or event.

Each letter is a pattern of movement or change in the One Life. Learning these patterns and developing a personal sense of what they are and how they work in your life is an important step toward wisdom. Over time, as you practice Coelbren divination, you will start to notice these patterns even when you aren't casting divinations, and you will be able to apply those insights in your readings and get even clearer and more accurate results.

∧ NAME: **A** (pronounced "Aah")

Meaning: Proceeding forward; continuation in the same state or condition, whether of motion, action, or rest

When this letter appears in a reading, it stands for a quality of easy onward movement. If the letter appears in the position that represents you, it is telling you to keep on doing what you've been doing and follow through in the direction you've already started going; if it represents another person for whom you are casting a reading, the same advice applies. If it appears in the position that represents the situation, it predicts that the situation that you are in will continue to behave in the same way that it's done up to this point; you don't need to worry that it will suddenly change direction or do something you don't expect. If it appears in the position representing the outcome, it predicts smooth sailing in general. Unless most of the other letters in the reading say otherwise, this letter is usually an indication of success.

⋁ NAME: *E* (pronounced "Eh")

Meaning: Motion checked, interrupted, or broken, an indirect, negative, or distorted condition

When this letter appears in a reading, it means that things are not going to continue in the way they appear to be going now. If the letter is in the position that represents you, it means that you will have to change direction or even, if the other letters in the reading support this interpretation, give up entirely on the project you have in mind. If it represents the situation that you are in, something you will encounter will act as an obstacle, forcing you to reconsider your approach and try something different; and if it represents the outcome, things will not turn out the way you expect. Whenever it appears in a reading, it shows that change is needed, and the other letters in the reading will help you determine what has to change and how you can redirect your efforts to achieve what you want out of the situation.

NAME: *I* (pronounced "Eee")

Meaning: The movement of a thing to its proper place, being or becoming a part of a whole, approach, applicability, subordination

When this letter appears in a reading, it means movement toward or into something—whether this is a good thing or not depends partly on the position the letter has in the reading, and partly on the nature of the question. If it turns up in an appropriate position in a reading about a relationship, for example, it's a strong indication that things will happen between the two people involved; if it appears in a reading about quitting your job, it likely means that you will be better off staying, because you are in the best place available to you, whether you realize it or not. In the position that represents you or another person for whom you are casting a reading, it tells you that going onward into whatever is under discussion is your best or even your only choice. In the positions that represent the situation or the outcome, this letter tells you that something new will be entering your life.

◇ NAME: **O** (pronounced "Oh")

Meaning: Movement outward or away from, departure, rejection or projection, casting or putting forth

When this letter appears in a reading, it lets you know that you can expect movement away from or out of something—again, whether this is a good thing or not depends on the position of the letter in the reading and the question that's been asked. If it represents you or another person for whom you are casting a reading, it may be telling you it's time to leave a situation that is no longer right for you. If it represents the situation, something that affects you is about to go away, and you will need to make other plans; if it represents the outcome, you will be leaving the situation whether you want to do so or not. Whatever it stands for in a reading will be going away, in one sense or another.

V NAME: **W** (pronounced "Ooo")

Meaning: Sorting or distributing things into different classes or categories, discrimination, divergence, choosing

When this letter appears in a reading, it tells you that a parting of the ways or a moment of choice is approaching you. Some things in your life will go one way and some will go a different way. If the letter represents you or another person for whom you are casting a reading, it may be telling you that you will need to make a choice between alternatives or to pay closer attention to the various options. If it represents the situation, it may mean that someone else will make a decision that affects you or that some other kind of division or sorting out will be taking place; and if it represents the outcome, things may go in more than one direction, and your actions will help determine what will happen. At its best, this letter tells you an abundance of possibilities, but it can also warn you that you will have to make your choice between alternatives and live with it.

Y NAME: **Y** (pronounced "Ih")

Meaning: A state or condition of balance or suspension, neutrality, pause, impartiality or uninvolvement

When this letter appears in a reading, it tells you that this is not the time to make a firm decision or take any action you cannot undo. If the letter is in a position that represents you, the advice it gives is to wait and put off any definite action for the time being; if it represents another person for whom you are casting the reading, the same advice applies. If it represents the situation, you can expect circumstances to keep something from happening; and if it represents the outcome, delay and inertia are the order of the day. This can be frustrating if it represents something that you want, but remember that it can also represent something that you don't want—in which case you don't have to worry about it happening immediately or depending on the other letters in the reading at all.

Y NAME: **U** (pronounced "Eeh")

Meaning: Wholeness, completeness, unity, the background or context in which other things or actions have their place

When this letter appears in a reading, it tells you that the situation is either already complete or is moving toward completion on its own, no matter what you do or don't do. If it represents you, it reminds you that you are part of a bigger picture than you may realize, and outside forces will have a larger impact on the outcome than anything you do or don't do. If it appears in the position that represents the situation, it suggests that one way or another, you (or another person for whom you are casting the reading) may not be able to do much to influence that part of the picture. If it appears in the position that represents the outcome, the question has already been settled and nothing you or anyone else can do will affect it.

NAME: *Bi* (pronounced "Bee")

Meaning: The being of anything in a resting state, a condition or state of being, mere existence, perception

When this letter appears in a reading, it means that things are what they are and will not change by themselves. If it shows up in a position that represents you, it means that you are going to keep on living the same life and experiencing the same things as before. The same meaning also applies, of course, if you're casting a reading for another person and this letter appears in a position representing that person. If it shows up in the position that represents the situation, the same rule applies—the situation isn't about to change—and when it shows up in the position that represents the outcome, it suggests that any efforts you make will have little if any effect. Depending on the other letters in the reading, this letter may mean that things aren't going to change until and unless you change them—or it may mean that things aren't going to change no matter what you do, and you probably need to learn to live with that.

NAME: *Ci* (pronounced "Kee")

Meaning: Holding, containing, comprehending, reaching or extension toward a thing, catching, attaining, and apprehending

When this letter appears in a reading, it indicates getting and holding. If you're casting a reading about whether you or another person can get something, such as a job or a romantic partner, the answer this letter gives is yes; if the question is whether you or another person can avoid getting something, such as an illness, the answer in that case is no! In a different position or in response to a different kind of question, it can mean that something is going to catch you or another person for good or ill. More broadly, it represents reaching or moving toward something; depending on the place in the reading where it appears, it can offer advice— "move toward this"—or give a warning—"this is coming toward you"—but in any case, the common theme of reaching and grasping remains the same.

> NAME: **Di** (pronounced "Dee")

Meaning: Expanding, unfolding, laying open, distribution and division, the opposite of Ci

When this letter appears in a reading, it indicates letting go and giving away. If it appears in a position that represents you or another person for whom you are casting a reading, it shows that it's time for you or the other person to let go of something. If the purpose of the reading is to find out if you can get something, the answer is therefore no—modified, of course, by the other letters in the reading—while if the issue under discussion is whether you can get over something or get out of something, the answer is yes. If this letter represents the situation, you can expect things to change, and if it represents the outcome, you can make them change.

ᚠ NAME: *Ffi* (pronounced "Fee")

Meaning: Cause, impulse, setting a thing or action in motion, the source or initial thrust of change or activity

When this letter appears in a reading, it tells you that things are going to have to be set in motion—they won't change unless something happens to make them change. If the letter appears in the position that represents you, it means that nothing is going to happen unless you do something, and if you're doing a reading for another person, that person should take the same advice. If it appears in the position that represents the situation, it shows you that something other than your actions and choices is driving the situation onward; and if it appears in the position that represents the outcome, it means that your actions will set things in motion.

〈   NAME: *Gi* (pronounced "Gee," with a hard G as in
gate or gas)

Meaning: Attachment, cohesion, appetite, desire, and also
compensation and mutual reaction of things on each other

When this letter appears in a reading, it tells you that the things
you are asking about are closely connected to one another, so that
changing one thing will change everything else. If it appears in
the position representing you or another person for whom you're
casting a reading, it suggests that any attempt to make things
happen will set off a cascade of changes with results you will not be
able to predict. This doesn't necessarily mean that doing so is a bad
idea, but you need to be prepared for the unexpected. If this letter
appears in the position that represents the situation, it cautions
you that there are connections and relationships in the situation
that you may not know about; and if it appears in the position that
represents the outcome, what's happening in the present situation
will have consequences that you may not be able to predict.

Ⱶ NAME: *Hi* (pronounced "Hee")

Meaning: Generation, abundance, fertility, nurturance, and support, response favorable to an external cause or stimulus

When this letter appears in a reading, it is a generally positive sign in most questions. If it appears in a position representing you or another person for whom you are casting a reading, it encourages a receptive and favorable approach to whatever events or actions the reading discusses. If it appears in the position that represents the situation, it predicts that the situation will be receptive to whatever you (or the person for whom you're casting a reading) are trying to do; and when it represents the outcome, it is a very good sign that things will go the way you want them to go. It generally indicates that things are favorable and, if supported by the other letters in the reading, is a promise of success.

ᛚ NAME: *Li* (pronounced "Lee")

Meaning: Flow, softness, smoothness, lightness, open space, solution or evanescence, movement without effort, as gliding

When this letter appears in a reading, it tells you that events are flowing smoothly, and your efforts are not needed to keep them moving. If the letter appears in the position that represents you or another person for whom you are casting a reading, it offers important advice: this is a good time to let things go the way they want to go, rather than trying to make them do what you think you want them to do. If it appears in the positions that represent the situation or the outcome, events are out of your control, and you simply have to accept that they're going to do what they're going to do. Unless other letters in the reading suggest otherwise, however, this is usually a favorable omen, suggesting that if things are allowed to go their own way, you or the person for whom you're casting the reading will be happy with the result.

W NAME: *Mi* (pronounced "Mee")

Meaning: Comprehending, embracing, or surrounding; enclosure or capacity, inclusion within something; large or complex

When this letter appears in a reading, it tells you that there is more going on than you realize, and you need to pay attention to the big picture rather than getting caught up in the details. When it appears in the position that represents you or another person for whom you are casting a reading, it suggests that whatever you do (or the other person does) will affect, and be affected by, many other people and things. Depending on the other letters in the reading, it may also indicate that you (or the other person) can accomplish your goals only as part of a group or that you or the other person are limited by the choices other people make. When it appears in the position that represents the situation, it lets you know that there is much more going on in the situation than you realize, and when it appears in the position that represents the outcome, what you do will have a much greater effect than you think. More generally, when this letter appears anywhere in a reading, it can also mean that the situation is much larger or more complex than it seems at first glance.

NAME: _Ni_ (pronounced "Nee")

Meaning: Distinguishing or identifying something; an individual object or subject; something new, simple, distinguished, or small

When this letter appears in a reading, it tells you that whatever it represents is the key to the entire situation. If it appears in the position that represents you, it tells you that your own choices and actions are the key to the entire situation; if you are casting a reading for someone else and the letter appears in a place representing that person, the same rule applies. If it appears in the position that represents the situation, you need to pay more attention to something other than yourself; and if it appears in the position that represents the outcome, it indicates that the problem is not as complicated as you think. More generally, this letter can also mean that the situation is much smaller or less complex than it appears.

↑ NAME: *Pi* (pronounced "Pee")

Meaning: Pushing, penetrating, springing, or putting forth; a protrusion or prominence, sharpness, convexity

When this letter appears in a reading, it tells you that things are about to change suddenly in some way. If it appears in the position representing you or another person for whom you're casting a reading, it means that you or that person will be responsible for the change and will be most strongly affected by it. If this letter appears in the position that represents the situation, then things will change suddenly no matter what you do; and if it appears in the position that represents the outcome, the change is still in the future and you may still have the option of keeping it from happening or guiding it the way you want it to go.

Ⲙ NAME: *Ri* (pronounced "Ree")

Meaning: Force, prevalence, or superiority; an action performed by main strength; excess, tearing or breaking, causing damage

When this letter appears in a reading, it tells you that the situation has gone too far to be dealt with by subtle or gentle measures; a major effort is going to be required. If it appears in the position that represents you, it suggests that forceful action on your part will be needed to get the results you hope for, but unless it is accompanied by very unfortunate letters, it also tells you that you have the strength to finish the job. If it represents another person for whom you're casting a reading, the same advice applies to that person. If it appears in the position that represents the situation, though, this letter is usually a bad sign and tells you that someone or something else has more power over the situation than you do and can be expected to use that strength in a forceful manner. If it appears in the position that represents the outcome, the other letters in the reading will tell you who will have the strength that it predicts.

ᛣ NAME: *Si* (pronounced "Shee")

Meaning: Inferiority, secrecy, privacy; a secret or private knowledge or indication; insinuation, indirect action

When this letter appears in a reading, it tells you that direct action is not an option and that going about things quietly and by indirect means is the way ahead. If it appears in the position that represents you, it means that you don't have enough power over the situation to take charge of the situation and therefore will have to use indirect means and avoid attracting notice in order to bring about the results you want. If it appears in the same position in a reading you're casting for another person, it very often means that the other person has not told you everything you need to know about the situation! If it appears in the position that represents the situation, there are hidden factors at work in the question; and if it appears in the position that represents the outcome, the results of the situation are still hidden, and you will just have to wait and see.

↑ NAME: *Ti* (pronounced "Tee")

Meaning: Tension, drawing, or straining; stretching or drawing out; bringing to an end; confinement or termination

When this letter appears in a reading, it tells you that something is coming to an end. If it appears in a position that represents you or another person for whom you are casting a reading, it very often means that the situation has gone too far for you or the other person to affect it. If it appears in the position that represents the situation, something in your situation will not last long. When it appears in the position that represents the outcome, it means that for good or ill, the situation is over, and you need to let go of it and proceed to other things. This letter can also represent tension and stress, and if it appears as your letter in a reading, you may need to spend more time relaxing.

ᚦ NAME: *Ddi* (pronounced "Thee")

Meaning: Realm, extent, or field of action; territory; boundary, surface, or interface marking the limit of a given force or influence

When this letter appears in a reading, it tells you the presence of a boundary that you may not be able to cross. If it appears in the position representing you, it tells you that your ability to affect the situation will only extend so far and very often advises you to pay attention to the difference between what you can influence and what you can't and focus on what you can actually do something about; if it represents another person for whom you're casting a reading, the same advice applies. If it appears in the position that represents the situation, it may mean that someone or something that concerns you will not affect you at all; while if it appears in the position that represents the outcome, you may be trying to do something that is out of your reach.

N NAME: *Lli* (pronounced "Hlee")

Meaning: Turbulence, confusion, and disruption; difficulty in proceeding; obstacles, solidity, movement requires effort

When this letter appears in a reading, it tells you that you are facing troubles, obstacles, and difficulties. If it appears in the position that represents you or another person for whom you're casting a reading, you will have a hard time accomplishing anything. If it appears in the position that represents the situation, the entire situation will be difficult; and if it appears in the position that represents the outcome, frustration and delay can be expected. Depending on the letters that appear with it, it may also simply indicate that a lot of things will be happening very fast, and you will find it hard to stay on track and avoid getting confused.

NAME: *Fi* (pronounced "Vee")

Meaning: Protection, limitation, discipline, establishment or maintenance of order; response unfavorable to an external cause

When this letter appears in a reading, it is a generally negative sign in most questions. If it appears in the position that represents you or another person for whom you are casting a reading, it warns you to take a cautious, wary attitude to whatever events or actions the reading discusses. If it appears in the position that represents the situation, you are facing a great deal of resistance and may not be able to achieve what you want; and if it appears in the position that represents the outcome, some outside factor or stimulus is likely to intervene and make things difficult for you. Whenever it appears, it warns you of trouble and tells you that you will need to be careful and watch for potential delays and difficulties.

K NAME: *Chi* (pronounced "Khee")

Meaning: Conflict, opposition, obstacle; mutual interference between two or more contending forces or things

When this letter appears in a reading, it tells you that some kind of struggle is coming. When it appears in the position that represents you or another person for whom you're casting a reading, it shows that you or the other person will have to struggle with obstacles or opposition to reach the desired goal. When it appears in the position that represents the situation, there is conflict all around you. Where Lli indicates complications, confusion, and difficulty, and Fi warns of resistance and delay, Chi tells you that active opposition of some kind is involved. Whether that opposition comes from a specific person, from impersonal forces, or from the sheer inertia of the situation, you are in for a fight.

RESOURCES FOR DIVINATION

Unless you know the Welsh language and have access to some fairly rare books, there is only one book on the Coelbren in print—*The Coelbren Alphabet: The Lost Oracle of the Welsh Bards*—which I wrote. It has more information about the history and meaning of the Coelbren, as well as many more spreads that can be used for divination. Not all Druids use the Coelbren letters, however! The Ogham (pronounced OH-um), which is an Irish symbolic alphabet dating from ancient times (shown below), also gets plenty of use among Druids as a tool for divination. There are many good books on Ogham divination in print nowadays, as well as several Ogham decks for sale, and some Druid organizations also teach Ogham divination to their students.

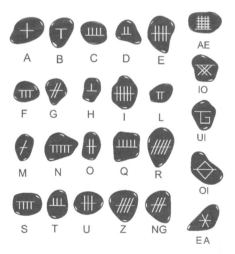

Two more recent decks that have become very popular among modern Druids are *The Druid Animal Oracle* and *The Druid Plant Oracle*, both by Philip and Stephanie Carr-Gomm, which use the animals or plants of Celtic tradition as basic symbols. There are many other Celtic- or Druid-themed divination decks available, some of them based on standard divination decks, such as the tarot or Lenormand deck. Others follow their own original pattern. As you follow your own Druid journey, consider exploring one or more of these alternative methods of divination and see how they work for you.

CHAPTER 11

Ritual

AS MENTIONED EARLIER IN THIS BOOK, THE three practices of observation, meditation, and divination, which have already been covered in this section, are all (in a certain sense) ways of listening. Observation is the art of listening to the One Life in the natural world; meditation is the art of listening to the One Life in teachings and symbols; and divination is the art of listening to the One Life directly, using the power of intuition. Learning to listen closely to all these things is an important part of Druidry.

Balancing these receptive practices is the active side of Druidry, which expresses itself especially in ritual. Ross Nichols, the most influential Druid thinker of the twentieth century, defined the art of ritual crisply in a single sentence: "Ritual is poetry in the world of acts." Poems are a symbolic form of language—they mean more than they say, and they communicate things that ordinary

language cannot. In exactly the same way, rituals are a symbolic form of action. What they mean is more important than what they do, and they can communicate in ways that go far beyond ordinary action.

It can be helpful to think of ritual as a performing art, like music or theater. It differs in one crucial way from other performing arts, however, for in ritual the performer and the audience are one and the same. One of the reasons that ritual has become so neglected in modern times is that too many ritualists forgot this and created rituals in which most people are assigned the role of passive spectator, sitting and watching while someone else does something. In Druid ritual, by contrast, there are no spectators. Everyone present takes at least a small part in the action.

The three rituals given in this book are meant for you to perform by and for yourself. The first of them, the Ritual of the Three Rays, is a rite of blessing and protection that you can do any time you wish. The second, the Ritual of the Druid Grove, is a method of establishing sacred space for some specific purpose and then, once the work is finished, returning the space to its normal condition. It includes the Ritual of the Three Rays. The third is a ritual of self-initiation that you can use to begin your Druid journey, and it includes the Ritual of the Three Rays and the Ritual of the Druid Grove. Because each ritual is included in the more complex rituals that come after it, the art of Druid ritual can be learned one step at a time.

RITUAL AND IMAGINATION

In order to understand Druid ritual, it's important to realize that the outward words and movements are only part, and not the most important part, of what goes on in a ritual working. Another part happens in the mind of the person or people doing the ritual. You can go through all the motions and say all the words of a ritual, in fact, and get no result, because you've left out the inner dimension that gives it power. It's as though you climbed into the driver's seat of a car and turned the key but forgot to make sure there was gas in the tank!

The fuel that makes a Druid ritual go somewhere and do something is provided by your imagination. These days, the imagination gets much less respect than it deserves. Consider the way that so many people nowadays use the word "imaginary" to mean "unreal." In actuality, of course, what we imagine is real in its own way, and it can be powerful and important as well. If you hear the footsteps of someone approaching your front door, and you think it's a robber who plans on breaking down the door

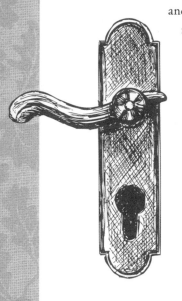

and holding you at gunpoint, your mind and body will react just as powerfully to that thought as it would to the actual presence of a robber. If you think instead that the footsteps are your own true love, come to give you a kiss, the reaction in your body and mind may be just as powerful, though of course it will be different!

What we imagine shapes how we experience the world, and it also shapes how we experience ourselves and who we become. This is what gives ritual its power—and that power is among the tools that Druids use.

As you begin practicing ritual, keep in mind that different people experience the imagination in different ways. Don't assume that you ought to be able to see the things you imagine as though there were a movie screen inside your head. (Some people have this ability, but most of us don't.) If you have trouble seeing something in your mind's eye, imagine what it would look like if you could see it clearly. Many people also find it useful to bring in other senses, and imagine what something would sound like, feel like, or even smell like. Instead of judging your imagination by some arbitrary standard, experiment with different approaches, try alternative ways of using your imagination, and see what works best for you.

THE RITUAL OF THE THREE RAYS

This is the most basic ritual in this book, and it is part of every other ritual you will practice as you work through this book. The only things you will need to perform it are yourself and a room or other private space, large enough that you can turn around in a circle with your arms held straight out without hitting anything. You will need to know the compass directions—you may be able to get those from a map on the internet, or you can use an inexpensive compass of the sort that campers and hikers carry with them. (Many Druids take one of these along when they travel, so they have no difficulty telling which direction is which in an unfamiliar place.)

The ritual is done in the following way:

FIRST, stand in the center of the space and face east. Imagine that the sun is high above you, shining its rays straight down upon you. Be aware of the earth beneath you, illuminated by the rays of the sun. Once you have imagined both of those as clearly as you can, draw in a deep breath, and as you do so, imagine a beam of golden light descending from the heart of the sun, passing through you, and going all the way to the heart of the earth. As you breathe out, hold that image in your mind and try to feel the beam of light passing through you on its way from sun to earth.

SECOND, let go of the previous image, and point to the east with the index finger of your right hand, holding your arm straight out. Say these words aloud: "May the east be blessed by the three rays of light." Then trace the symbol of the three rays of light in the air, as though drawing it with the tip of your finger. Draw the left-hand ray first, then the right-hand ray, and then the central ray, as shown in the diagram below.

As you trace each line with your finger, imagine that it becomes a line of golden light drawn in the air in front of you.

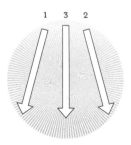

THIRD, now point to the east again with your right index finger, holding your arm straight out. Turn slowly to face south, and as you do this, imagine that your finger is tracing a line of golden light as it moves. Once you are pointing toward the south, trace the three rays of light in the air to the south exactly as you did to the east, imagining the lines drawn in golden light, and say these words aloud: "May the south be blessed by the three rays of light."

FOURTH, repeat the same process, turning to the west, imagining that your finger draws a line of golden light as you turn, and tracing the three rays in light toward the west. Say these words aloud: "May the west be blessed by the three rays of light."

FIFTH, repeat the same process, turning to the north and doing all the same steps there as you did in the other three quarters. Say these words aloud: "May the north be blessed by the three rays of light."

SIXTH, turn to face east again, imagining that your finger draws a line of golden light to connect to the place where you first pointed. In your imagination, you are now standing inside a circle of golden light that hovers in the air around you, with the symbol of the three rays of light traced in each of the four directions, as shown in the diagram below.

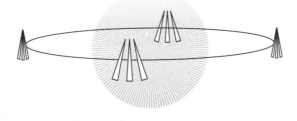

SEVENTH, hold your arms angled outward and downward to your sides, so that your arms and body form the symbol of the three rays of light. Chant the sacred word of the Druid Revival tradition, AWEN. Pronounce it in three syllables, AH-OO-EN. As you chant AH, be aware of the sky above you, the sun shining, if it is daytime, and the stars, if it is night. As you chant OO, be aware of the earth beneath you. As you chant EN, be aware of yourself standing between earth and sky, a very small part of a very big universe. When you have finished chanting the word, lower your arms and release the imagery. This completes the Ritual of the Three Rays.

Simple as it is, this ritual contains a great deal of symbolism. The One Life, the two currents, the three rays of light, and the four elements are all part of it. So are three letters of the Coelbren! The grand word Awen is traditionally written ∧ ∨ ∕∖, AWN, and if you meditate on the letter *A* as a symbol of the skies, the letter *W* as a symbol of the earth, and the letter *Ni* as a symbol of yourself, you will understand a little more about the ritual, the Coelbren letters, and the universe in which you live.

Practice the Ritual of the Three Rays regularly until you can do it from memory, without having to use this book or a cheat sheet to remind you what to do next. Once you have learned it, practicing it every week is a good idea, and once a day is not too often; many Druids find that it works well to do this or a similar ritual just before meditation, so they can meditate in a space that has been blessed and protected by the power of imagination. When you can do the ritual easily from memory without mistakes, go on to learn the Ritual of the Druid Grove.

THE RITUAL OF THE DRUID GROVE

In the traditions of the Druid Revival, a space where Druids meet to perform ritual is called a grove. Originally, of course, the name was literally true—one of the things that ancient Greek and Roman travelers recorded about the ancient Druids is that they practiced at least some of their ceremonies in groves of trees—but as the modern Druid movement developed, the term came to be used more broadly. Now any space, with or without trees, indoors or out, where Druids meet can be a grove, and as you have already learned, "grove" is also a common name for a local Druid group.

The grove you will establish in this ritual is your personal Druid grove, a sacred space in which you can perform various kinds of ritual work—above all, your self-initiation as a Druid. You will need a somewhat larger space than the minimum for the Ritual of the Three Rays of Light: enough room that you can put a chair in the center and walk in a circle around it without bumping into anything.

You will also need four small bowls or cauldrons: pottery bowls a few inches across will serve, and so will brass cauldrons of the same size, the sort that can be bought at many import shops. These will become symbols of the four elements. Before the ritual, one of the bowls should be half full of water, and a second should be half full of dry soil or little stones. If your living situation allows you to use fire in your rituals, the third bowl should be partly full of sand, so that you can burn incense in it safely—cone incense works well in this ritual, and so does short stick incense. (Long sticks tend to fall over.) The fourth bowl, if you can use fire, contains a votive candle. If for some reason you need to avoid open flame, the third bowl or cauldron should contain a potpourri of scented dry flowers and herbs, and the fourth should contain a crystal, which represents light. Set the four bowls or cauldrons around the outside of your working space, as shown in the diagram on the opposite page, with the bowl of incense or potpourri to the east, the bowl of fire or crystal to the south, the bowl of water to the west, and the bowl of earth or stones to the north. (In the ritual, as you have no doubt guessed already, these are called the Cauldron of Air, the Cauldron of Fire, the Cauldron of Water, and the Cauldron of Earth, respectively.) If you will be doing a meditation in your grove, or any other form of work that is best done sitting, a chair should be placed a little to the west of the center of the circle, facing east. Once everything that you need is in place, light the incense and the candle, if you are using them, and you are ready to begin.

Opening the Grove

The ritual for opening the grove is performed as follows:

FIRST, stand in the center of the space—just in front of the chair if you are using one—and face east. Pause for a moment and clear your mind. Then say aloud: "In the presence of the powers of nature I prepare to open a grove of Druids. Let peace be proclaimed to the four quarters." Step to the east, stopping just short of the Cauldron of Air, and raise your right hand, palm out, as though you were greeting someone who was a long distance away. Say aloud: "May there be peace in the east."

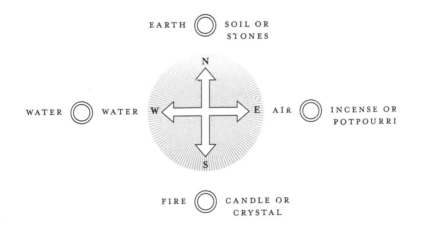

SECOND, circle around to the south, face south, raise your hand in greeting, and say, "May there be peace in the south." Circle to the west and do the same thing, saying, "May there be peace in the west." Repeat to the north, saying, "May there be peace in the north." Circle around to the east and then return to the center and face east.

Proclaiming peace to the four quarters is the traditional first step in Druid ritual and is included in the ceremonies of many different Druid traditions, though not all of them do it in exactly the same way. In Wales, during the Middle Ages, it was strictly forbidden to draw a weapon at an assembly of bards, and the proclamation of peace was meant to announce that this rule was in effect. Among Druids nowadays, the proclamation of peace is meant to remind everyone present to set aside any distracting thoughts or upset feelings and turn their thoughts and efforts to the ritual that is about to be performed.

THIRD, do the complete Ritual of the Three Rays. Instead of turning in place, when it is time to begin tracing lines, go to the eastern edge of the space, trace the three rays there, and then circle around the outside of the space to the south, the west, the north, and back to the east, tracing the circle around the whole space where the ritual will take place, before returning to the center. All your other work in this ritual should take place inside the circle you trace in this step.

FOURTH, go to the east again and pick up the Cauldron of Air. Face east, hold the Cauldron up as though in offering, and say, "Let this grove and all within it be blessed and protected by the element of Air." Then walk slowly around the space, carrying the Cauldron of Air with you, and imagine that a fresh breeze swirls around with you as you walk, cleansing and protecting the space. Set the Cauldron of Air down when you complete the circle in the east.

FIFTH, go to the south and pick up the Cauldron of Fire. Face south, hold the Cauldron up as though in offering, and say, "Let this grove and all within it be blessed and protected by the element of Fire." Then walk slowly around the space, carrying the Cauldron of Fire with you, and imagine that flames rise around you as you walk, cleansing and protecting the space. Set the Cauldron of Fire down when you complete the circle in the south.

SIXTH, go to the west and pick up the Cauldron of Water. Face west, hold the Cauldron up as though in offering, and say, "Let this grove and all within it be blessed and protected by the element of Water." Then walk slowly around the space, carrying the Cauldron of Water with you, and imagine that rain pours down around you as you walk, cleansing and protecting the space. Set the Cauldron of Water down when you complete the circle in the west.

SEVENTH, go to the north and pick up the Cauldron of Earth. Face north, hold the Cauldron up as though in offering, and say, "Let this grove and all within it be blessed and protected by the element of Earth." Then walk slowly around the space, carrying the Cauldron of Earth with you, and imagine that the scent of rich, freshly turned earth rises around the space as you walk, cleansing and protecting the space. Set the Cauldron of Earth down when you complete the circle, returning to the north.

EIGHTH, return to the center and face east. Repeat the Druid Prayer, which is given on page 158. It is traditional and appropriate for you to replace the words "O Spirit" in the first and last lines, and elsewhere in the Ritual of the Druid Grove, with the name of the Divinity you use in your personal worship if you are a person who practices a particular religion: for example, Christian Druids begin this prayer "Grant, O God . . ." or "Grant, O Lord Jesus . . ." while Pagan Druids very often say "Grant, O Gods and Goddesses . . ." or "Grant, O holy powers . . ." The prayer runs as follows:

"Grant, O Spirit, your protection,
And in protection, strength,
And in strength, understanding,
And in understanding, knowledge,
And in knowledge, the knowledge of justice,
And in the knowledge of justice, the love of it,
And in that love, the love of all existences,
And in the love of all existences, the love of Spirit and all goodness."

NINTH, pause, and then say aloud, "In the presence of Spirit and the powers of nature, I declare that this grove of Druids is open." This completes the opening ritual, and you can then go on to do whatever you plan on doing in the open grove. (Some suggestions for things you can do in an open grove will be given a little later in this section.)

Closing the Grove

Once you have finished the work you have in mind, you should always close the grove. The ritual for closing the grove is performed as follows:

FIRST, standing in the center of the space, facing east, say aloud, "In the presence of the powers of nature I prepare to close this grove of Druids."

SECOND, go to the east and pick up the Cauldron of Air in both hands. Facing east, raise the Cauldron up as though in offering, and say aloud, "I thank the element of Air for its blessing and protection." Imagine the element of Air swirling in the east. Then set the Cauldron back down. You do not need to carry it around the circle as you did in the opening.

THIRD, go to the south and pick up the Cauldron of Fire in both hands. Facing east, raise the Cauldron up as though in offering, and say aloud, "I thank the element of Fire for its blessing and protection." Imagine the element of Fire blazing in the south. Then set the Cauldron back down.

FOURTH, go to the west and pick up the Cauldron of Water in both hands. Facing east, raise the Cauldron up as though in offering, and say aloud, "I thank the element of Water for its blessing and protection." Imagine the element of Water flowing and splashing in the west. Then set the Cauldron back down.

FIFTH, go to the north and pick up the Cauldron of Earth in both hands. Facing east, raise the Cauldron, as though in offering, and say aloud, "I thank the element of Earth for its blessing and protection." Imagine the element of Earth strong and stable in the north. Then set the Cauldron back down.

SIXTH, go to the center of the space, face east, and say aloud, "As this work began in peace, so let it end in peace. In the presence of Spirit and the powers of nature, I declare that this grove of Druids is closed." (Here again, as in the opening, you can replace the word "Spirit" with a name of Divinity if you wish.) This completes the closing ritual.

Like the Ritual of the Three Rays, the Ritual of the Druid Grove has plenty of symbolism and Druid teaching woven into it and will repay study and meditation—and, of course, regular practice! You will need to be able to perform it smoothly and effectively from memory, without looking at this book or a cheat sheet, before you will be ready to perform the ritual of self-initiation covered in the final section of this book.

RITUALS FOR TWO OR MORE

If you know other people who are interested in practicing Druidry with you, you may wish to do ritual work together from time to time. Three things will help you make the most of group ritual. The first is that everyone who participates should know how to do the solitary versions of the rituals from memory and should keep on practicing the solitary versions in order to develop their skills further. The second is that the rituals should be divided up into roughly equal parts, so that everyone has a share in the work, and no one is stuck in the role of a spectator, watching while someone else does the ritual. The third is that it helps to practice any ritual work informally as a group several times, so that everyone knows what to do and when to do it, before working that ritual for any other purpose.

An example may help clarify how this works. Let's say that you and one other person decide that you want to practice Druid rituals together. Both of you should practice the Ritual of the Three Rays of Light and the Ritual of the Druid Grove on your own until you can both do them from memory. You can then divide up the work of the rituals between you. For instance, with two people, it works well to have one person do the parts of each ritual that are done standing at the center, and the other do the parts that are done at the outer edge of the space. It's usually a good idea for you to alternate, so that whoever did the work at the center in one ritual working does the work at the outer edge the next time, and vice versa. Walk through the rituals a few times, alternating which of you does which part, and you should be ready to do effective ritual work together.

What if there are more people involved? The same principles apply. If you are one of a group of five friends who have decided to follow the Druid path together, for example, it works well to have one person do the parts of the ritual that are done in the center and have each of the other four take charge of one of the four directions and elements. When you do the Ritual of the Three Rays, the person in the middle imagines the sun, and keeps that image in place all through the working. The person in the east traces the three rays of light and says the words to the east. The person in the south then comes to the east, draws a line a quarter of the way around the space to the south, traces the three rays of light and says the words to the south. The person in the west does the same thing, coming to the south, drawing the line from there, tracing the sign and saying the words, and the person in the north then does the same. Finally the person in the east goes to the north and traces the line to complete the last quarter of the circle. Here again, it is usually a good idea to alternate roles, so that everyone gets familiar with every part, and so each of you has the chance to work with each of the elements in turn.

Remember that some words gain power when spoken by more than one person. The sacred word Awen should always be chanted aloud by everyone present at a Druid ritual. The Druid Prayer is also traditionally spoken, when Druids are performing ritual together, in a particular way that combines solo and group recitation. One person begins it, but the words shown below **in black** are repeated together by all present:

"*Grant, O Spirit, your protection,*
And in protection, strength,
And in strength, understanding,
And in understanding, knowledge,
And in knowledge, the knowledge of justice,
And in the knowledge of justice, the love of it,
And in that love, the love of all existences,
And in the love of all existences, the love of Spirit and all goodness."

Anything spoken by more than one person at the same time should be recited a little more slowly than usual, so that everyone can say the words together. A few practice sessions will make it easy for your group to do this together.

WORKING IN THE DRUID GROVE

Once you know how to perform the Ritual of the Three Rays of Light and the Ritual of the Druid Grove, and you can do them from memory, you will have a set of Druid rituals that you can use for many different purposes, either by yourself or together with others. Among the things that Druids do between the opening and closing halves of a grove ritual are these:

Celebrating the Seasons

Most Druids celebrate either four or eight holidays a year: either the two solstices and two equinoxes, or those plus the "cross quarter days" of Candlemas, May Day, Lammas, and All Hallows. The full set is shown in the table below. (Note: The dates here correspond to the Northern Hemisphere.)

DATE	COMMON NAME	WELSH NAME	PRONUNCIATION	ALTERNATE NAME
DEC 21	Winter Solstice	Alban Arthan	AL-ban AR-than	–
FEB 2	Candlemas	Calan Myri	CAH-lan MIH-ree	Imbolc
MAR 21	Spring Equinox	Alban Eilir	Al-ban EYE-lir	–
MAY 1	May Day	Calan Mai	CAH-lan MY	Belteinne
JUNE 22	Summer Solstice	Alban Hefin	AL-ban HEV-in	–
AUG 1	Lammas	Calan Gwyngalaf	CAH-lan GWIN-gal-av	Lughnasadh
SEP 22	Autumn Equinox	Alban Elfed	AL-ban EL-ved	–
NOV 1	All Hallows	Calan Tachwedd	CAH-lan TAKH-weth	Samhuinn

In many Druid organizations it is usual to have a grove meeting on each of the holidays and perform a ritual, a group meditation, or some other activity to celebrate the turning of the seasons. Some groups like to perform complicated, scripted rituals with many props and symbolic speeches, while others prefer simpler and more spontaneous activities.

Once you have done the self-initiation ritual to mark the beginning of your journey on the Druid path, you can use the grove ceremony as a framework for your own seasonal celebrations. Those can be as simple or as complex as you yourself choose to make them. On the less complicated end of the spectrum, for example, you might spend the weeks before each of the Druid holidays choosing two or three poems or short pieces of prose writing that you consider relevant to the season; after you open the grove, read those aloud one at a time, and then meditate on the season that is beginning and what lessons it has to teach you. Quiet and simple as this form of ritual is, you will find that it can be deeply moving and meaningful and can enhance both your experience of the seasons and your work as a Druid.

Studying Druidry

Some Druid organizations recommend that students open a grove once each week and, in the open grove, read a lesson or part of a book on Druidry, then meditate on the ideas in the lesson or the book. This is a practice worth exploring, and many Druids take it up as a regular part of their path. Inside the sacred space of a grove that has been opened by ritual, the mind is more open to the influences of spirit. If you decide to join a Druid organization that has lessons or written teachings, you can use these as the focus of this kind of work. If you continue to follow the Druid path on your own, simply choose a book of Druid philosophy and teaching, and read a few pages of it in an open grove once a week. You will be surprised to discover how much you learn in this way.

Working with Imagination

This is an important part of many spiritual paths because your imagination has potentials that most people never explore, or even notice. These days, as mentioned earlier, many people forget that imagination is the starting place for all human action, and that everything human beings have ever done or made or accomplished had to exist in someone's imagination first before it took shape in the world of matter. To work with your imagination is to come into contact with the sources of creativity and innovation. It is to approach the wellsprings of your own personal Awen.

Many Druids thus make time regularly to work with the imagination. One of the most widely used ways of doing this is to open a Druid grove using the ritual you have just learned, making sure you have a chair in the center of the space.

Once you have finished the opening ritual, sit down and go through the same process you would use if you were preparing to meditate: relax your body, and then spend a few minutes in the Fourfold Breath. Once you are ready to go on, instead of concentrating on a theme, imagine that you are in a clearing in the middle of a forest. Tall trees rise all around you, but you can see the sky directly above. Take some time to imagine the scene as clearly as you can. What kinds of trees surround you? Is the sky clear or cloudy, and what time of day is it? Imagine yourself standing up and

walking around the clearing; smell the scents of the forest and the ground beneath your feet, and hear the wind rustling in the leaves.

This clearing is your own private Druid grove in the realms of the imagination. You can go there any time you want by performing the opening half of the Ritual of the Druid Grove, sitting on your chair, and imagining yourself there. Once you've gone there several times, you can begin using it to work with the imagination by meeting imaginary people and beings in the grove and by going on imaginary journeys that begin and end at the grove.

To meet imaginary people in your grove, perform the opening ritual and go to your grove. Then simply imagine the person you want to meet coming out of the forest to greet you. Let's say that you have been studying and meditating on the legends of King Arthur and decide to make contact with Merlin in this way. Go to your grove and imagine Merlin coming to meet you there. Picture him in your mind's eye as clearly as you can; notice the shape of his face and hands, the color and cut of his hair and beard, the clothing he is wearing, and so on. Welcome him as though he were a real person and imagine yourself having a conversation with him. You may be surprised by what he says to you!

One of the secrets of the creative imagination is that the figures you imagine often behave as though they have a life of their own, and since the imagination links down into the unconscious mind, they can know things that you have forgotten or never realized you knew. (Many writers of fiction use the imagination in exactly this way to make their characters more lifelike and interesting.)

When the conversation is finished, thank him and say farewell, and wait until he has gone back into the forest before returning from your imaginary grove and performing the closing ritual.

To go on an imaginary journey, start the same way. Instead of having someone come to meet you, however, imagine a path leading through the forest away from your grove. Imagine yourself getting up from your chair and leaving the grove, walking along the path just as you would if you were on a path in the material world. Imagine the things around you as clearly as you are able. You can simply wander for a time and then go back to your

grove or you can have a destination in mind. Since all this is taking place in your imagination, you can go anywhere in space or time. If you want to take an imaginary journey to Stonehenge in the days of the ancient Druids, for example, you can certainly do that. Always remember to return to your grove once your journey is done.

One further caution is worth making here. What is real in the world of the imagination can inspire you to accomplish things in the world of everyday life, but it can be a mistake to take it too seriously too soon. Your imaginary conversations and journeys, like dreams and visions, can offer you insights into your life and much more, but if you take what you experience there literally, you can make a fool of yourself, or worse. Do you recall all those predictions that the world was going to end on December 21, 2012? Many of the people who made those predictions, or believed them, lost track of the difference between the world of imagination and the world of everyday life. Some of the things that you experience in your imagination can also happen here and now, *but you have to make them happen.* This is how books get written, songs get composed, technologies get invented, and organizations get founded; it's how people discover that they aren't satisfied with the way that they are living their lives and figure out how to do something different instead.

This is also how the Druid Revival came into being three hundred years ago. Imagining a Druid spirituality for the modern world was the essential first step in making the Revival happen, but it was only the first step. The steps that followed involved plenty of reading, meditation, learning from nature, performing rituals, talking with other people, starting organizations, and much more, so that the dream of a Druid Revival could become a reality. Those same steps are part of the work that waits for you, if you choose to complete the course of study and practice given in this book and initiate yourself as a Druid.

PART FOUR

INITIATION INTO DRUIDRY

SOME RELIGIONS AND SOME SPIRITUAL PATHS GAIN new members by conversion, but I have never known anyone who converted to Druidry. What happens instead is that people realize that they have been Druids all along. Some people find out about Druidry by reading a book or a website or by talking to a Druid and then say, "You know, that's what I've always felt like—I just didn't know that there was a word for it." Others find Druidry in some similar way, decide that it seems interesting, and experiment with it a little at a time—a ritual here, a meditation there, some time spent outdoors—and notice after a while that these practices add something to their lives that makes a difference to them.

If either of these descriptions applies to you, you may wish to consider performing the ritual of initiation given in this book, which will mark the beginning of your journey on the Druid path. You aren't required to perform an initiation ritual to become a Druid, but many people who take up Druidry find that a ceremony of this kind is worth doing as a way of marking what is often an important turning point in their lives.

A few points are worth making here. First of all, there's a remarkably large amount of nonsense about initiation rituals in circulation these days, mostly passed around by people who have never seen or experienced one. You aren't going to be asked to take dreadful oaths, invoke evil spirits, or sign a pledge in blood—or even in ink! Your initiation is a ritual in the sense already discussed in this book: "poetry in the realm of acts," in the words of Ross Nichols. It is a set of words, actions, and imaginations that is meant to have an effect on the way you experience yourself and the world. If you are a religious person, you are encouraged to invoke Divinity during the ritual to request a blessing and protection for your work as a Druid and to include, in the initiation ritual, the name by which you call on Divinity and the scriptures and symbols of your religious faith.

The mistaken notion that initiation rituals involve dreadful oaths to sinister powers is balanced by the equally mistaken notion that initiation rituals confer strange powers or give you the right to boast about being an initiate. If you expect strange powers from the ritual that follows or from any other ritual, you're going to be disappointed, for the subtle abilities of the mind that are at the root of all those stories about strange powers have to be developed by the steady, patient practice of meditation and certain other spiritual exercises—you don't get them just by going through a ritual! If you swagger around, claiming to be an initiate and a Druid once you've done the ritual that follows, for that matter, you're just going to look silly, and a few years from now you'll cringe as you realize how many people were laughing at you once you were out of earshot. Being a Druid doesn't make you more special than anybody else. It simply means that you've decided to follow a certain tradition of seeking wisdom in nature.

A third caution that should be made here is that many Druid organizations have their own initiation rituals, and the ritual that follows is not a substitute for those. When I became a Druid in 1994, I received the initiation of the Bardic Grade, the first of three grades that are conferred by the Order of Bards Ovates and Druids and went on to receive the other two once I qualified for them. When I became a member of the Ancient Order of Druids in America in 2003, I received the Candidate Initiation, followed by the initiations of three further degrees, and the fact that I had already been initiated as a Druid didn't exempt me from having to earn each of those further initiations. In the same way, if you decide to join a Druid organization that has its own teachings and initiations, you will need to study those teachings and receive those initiations if you want to benefit fully from your membership. The fact that you've performed the initiation in this book is no replacement for that.

If you understand these things, you are ready to begin preparing for your initiation as a Druid. Your journey is about to begin. . . .

CHAPTER 12

Preparing
for Your
Initiation

BEFORE YOU CAN PERFORM THE RITUAL OF self-initiation given in this book, you need to become familiar with all the symbols and teachings covered in part two, and you need to learn and experience all the practices given in part three. If you just fumble your way through the ritual first without doing any of the necessary preparation, it won't accomplish anything for you. If you take the time to prepare for it properly, on the other hand, it will become a meaningful experience to mark the beginning of your journey as a Druid.

Plan on spending at least seven weeks preparing for your initiation. During that period, at least seven times practice observation, sitting quietly where you can see the world of nature and paying attention to it. During those same seven weeks do each of the exercises to bring yourself into contact with the two currents and four elements at least once and meditate at least once

on the One Life, each of the two currents, each of the three rays of light, and each of the four elements. (This will take you a minimum of six outdoor exercises and ten sessions of meditation.)

During those seven weeks cast and interpret at least seven Coelbren readings and then review them and see whether you can understand more of what they were saying to you. During those same seven weeks learn and practice the Ritual of the Three Rays and the Ritual of the Grove until you can do both of them from memory without having to refer to this book or a cheat sheet to remind you what you're supposed to do next. Finally, at some point during those seven weeks create your own Druid grove in the realm of the imagination, as explained on pages 166–70, and go there often enough that you can return there easily. Part of the ritual of initiation that follows will take place there.

Can you do the minimum amount of work needed to prepare for your initiation in less than seven weeks? Of course, but take the full seven weeks anyway and do more observation, meditation, divination, and ritual as time permits. If you have the spare time and the enthusiasm, you can do each of these practices every day for seven weeks—and if you do that, your initiation will be even more powerful and meaningful to you.

REQUIREMENTS OF THE RITUAL

To perform your ritual of self-initiation you will need a private place, indoors or outside, where you can be sure you will not be interrupted for at least an hour. It is traditional to do this ritual outdoors in the daytime—"in the face of the Sun, the eye of light," as some old Druid rituals phrase it—

but your circumstances may or may not permit this. Choose a time and a place that works for you.

You will need certain things to perform the ritual. The four cauldrons of the elements you learned to use in the Ritual of the Druid Grove are among these, and so are two chairs, one to place at the center of your working space and one to place somewhere outside the circle you will trace. Your Coelbren set is also needed because you will be casting a reading during the ceremony, and you should have paper and a pen to write down the reading so you can refer to it in the future. You will also need a large stone—anything larger than a pebble will do, but the larger it is, the better—and a bowl of clean water, which should be larger than your Cauldron of Water. (These represent a standing stone and a sacred well. If you can do the ritual someplace where there is a standing stone next to a well or spring, and you can trace your circle so that those are in the east, this would be best of all, but few of us have that option.)

Put the four cauldrons of the elements in the four quarters, one of the chairs in the center of the circle, your Coelbren set near that chair, and the stone and bowl of water in the east, alongside the Cauldron of Air. The other chair should go near the circle, but in a position so that you cannot see the circle. If you are doing the ritual outdoors, put it a short distance from the circle, facing away; if you will be inside, the chair can simply go in the next room. Be sure you have water in the Cauldron of Water and the bowl, and if you use incense and a candle, have matches or a lighter handy!

If you wish, you can decorate the space in any way that is meaningful to you, with flowers in spring, fallen leaves in the autumn, or what have you. If you are a religious person, the sacred scriptures of your faith and any images, statues, or symbols that are important in your religion

can certainly be included; you will also want to choose one or two short passages from sacred writings to read aloud during the ceremony. (Among Christian Druids, the Bible text that is typically used for initiation into Druidry is the first five verses of the first chapter of the Gospel of John, but if you decided you would rather use a different text, by all means do so.) If you don't have any text you would like to read, simply use the one given below in the ritual.

If you want to wear a traditional white robe for this initiation, by all means do so. If you would rather follow the old Druid Revival custom of tying a colored ribbon around your right arm, a green ribbon would be appropriate, as this was used in those days to mark the first step in Druidry.

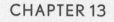

CHAPTER 13

A Ritual of Self-Initiation

ONCE YOU HAVE THE TIME, THE PLACE, AND the things you need, you are ready to begin. Set up the circle as just described, and then leave it and go to the chair you have put outside the circle. Sit down and spend some time thinking about what you are about to do. Call to mind everything you have learned about Druidry from this book and any other books on the subject that you may have read. Realize that you are about to make Druidry part of your life and that you will have to set aside time and energy for it from now on if you are going to gain anything from becoming a Druid.

When you feel you are ready, rise from the chair and go into the circle. Light the incense in the east and the candle in the south if you are using these. Stand in the center of the circle in front of the chair, facing east. Pause to clear your mind and ready yourself for the ritual you are about to perform and then begin.

FIRST, perform the complete ritual for opening a Druid grove, exactly as it was described in the previous section of this book (see pages 155–58).

SECOND, once the grove is open, sit on the chair and read aloud the text from sacred writings that you have chosen or the following text from Druid lore. (You may also do both if you wish.) Read the text slowly and attentively, thinking about the meanings of the words and the text as you read it.

"In the beginning of time, Einigan the Giant, the first of all created beings, saw three rays of light descending from the heavens, which had in them all the knowledge that ever was or ever will be. He took three staves of rowan wood and carved on the branches the forms of signs of all knowledge so that none of it would be forgotten. In time, however, those who saw the rowan staves misunderstood and worshiped them as gods instead of learning from the knowledge written on them. When he saw this, Einigan was greatly distressed. So great was his grief that he burst into pieces, and after his death the rowan staves were lost.

"When a year and a day had passed since the death of Einigan, Menw son of Teirwaedd happened across the skull of Einigan and found that the three rowan staves had taken root and were growing out of the mouth of the skull. He found that by careful study he was able to read some of the writing on the staves. From the lore that he learned, Menw became the first of the gwyddons, the loremasters of the Celts in the most ancient times, before the Druids, and it was from the gwyddons that the secrets of the three rays of light were passed down to the Druids who came after them."

If you wish, you may also say a prayer at this point in the ritual, asking for guidance and blessing in your work as a Druid. This should be done right after the reading.

THIRD, sit for a time in silence, and then stand up and face east. Say aloud: "I ask the element of Air to be present to bless and witness my initiation as a Druid." Turn to face south, and say, "I ask the element of Fire to be present to bless and witness my initiation as a Druid." Turn to face west and say, "I ask the element of Water to be present to bless and witness my initiation as a Druid." Turn to face north and say, "I ask the element of Earth to be present to bless and witness my initiation as a Druid."

FOURTH, turn to face east again and then go to the east, where the stone and water have been placed. Kneel or sit on the ground and place your right hand upon the stone. Say aloud: "By this stone I make and renew every covenant that is made between heaven and the world of nature. May the solar current be awakened and may it bless my initiation as a Druid." Pause and imagine the solar current streaming down from the heavens to the earth. Imagine that you can feel it flowing through you, sustaining your life and your spirit. Spend a short time being aware of this.

FIFTH, dip three fingers of your left hand into the water, bring the fingers to your face, and draw them down your forehead, spreading them as you do so, to trace the sign of the three rays of light, / | \ , on your skin.

Say aloud: "By this water I make and renew every covenant that is made between earth and the world of nature. May the telluric current be awakened and may it bless my initiation as a Druid." Pause and imagine the telluric current streaming up from the earth to the heavens. Imagine that you can feel it flowing through you, sustaining your life and your spirit. Spend a short time being aware of this.

SIXTH, rise and return to the chair at the center of the circle. Sit down and enter your personal Druid grove in the realm of imagination in the way you have learned. When you have finished entering the grove and can sense it clearly around you, imagine three wise Druids approaching you out of the forest. Take some time to imagine the Druids clearly—are they old or young, female or male? What do they wear and what do they carry with them? Greet them as you would greet three wise elders who have come to teach you.

"Welcome," the Druids say to you. Then one of them asks you, "Will you follow the Druid path to the best of your ability?" You answer in your own words.

The second Druid asks you, "Will you seek for wisdom in your own way?" You answer in your own words.

The third Druid asks you, "Will you listen for the voice of your own Awen?" You answer in your own words.

"It is well," say each of the Druids, one after another. Then two of them take your hands in theirs, and the third, standing in the middle, places a hand on the top of your head. "We receive you and welcome you as a Druid," says the one in the middle, "and we bless you with the blessing of the One Life, that your senses may be open, your mind clear, and your spirit awake. The world of nature is waiting to teach you its lessons. Go forth and learn." Thank them in your own words, say farewell to them, and wait until they have returned to the forest, and then return from your grove of the imagination.

SEVENTH, cast a Coelbren reading. This is a special reading, and though it uses three letters like the spread you have been using, you put them down in a different order and they have different meanings. The first one goes in the center and represents you. The second goes to the right and represents the things that will help you along your Druid path. The third goes to the left and represents the things you have yet to learn on your Druid path. The diagram below shows you this spread.

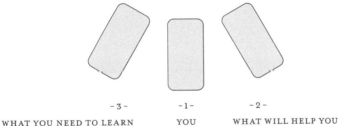

- 3 -	- 1 -	- 2 -
WHAT YOU NEED TO LEARN	YOU	WHAT WILL HELP YOU

Once you have cast the reading, write it down and think about what it tells you about the first stages of the path ahead of you.

EIGHTH, once you have finished thinking about your divination, rise to your feet. Realize that you are a Druid, a seeker after the wisdom in nature, an heir to the legacy of the Druid Revival following in the footsteps of the Druids of ancient times. Spread your arms wide and chant the word

Awen three times, drawing it out as you have been taught: AH-OO-EN. As you chant AH, be aware of the skies above you. As you chant OO, be aware of the earth beneath you. As you chant EN, be aware of yourself standing between earth and sky. When you have chanted the word three times, lower your arms.

NINTH, perform the ritual to close a Druid grove, exactly as you have learned to do it. This completes your ritual of self-initiation.

EPILOGUE

AFTER YOUR INITIATION

The word "initiation" literally means "beginning," and your initiation into Druidry is exactly that. You have learned a little of the lore of the Druid Revival tradition and experienced a few of the basic practices of Druidry. What this means is simply that you have taken your first step in the quest for wisdom in nature that has inspired modern Druids for three hundred years. The ritual of initiation you have passed through marks the completion of that first step . . . and the beginning of the next one.

There are many good books on Druidry that will help you take that next step, and there are also organizations that can help you learn more about Druidry; some of both are included in the resources section at the end of this book, along with some of the divination methods that are popular among Druids today. A more important source of guidance than books and organizations, however, is the time you spend working with the basic practices of Druidry, listening to the One Life, and learning from nature. No one can do that for you. The only thing that limits how much you can learn and grow on the adventure of Druidry is your own willingness to pursue it.

Your Druid journey has begun. May the One Life, the two currents, the three rays of light, and the four elements bless and guide you as you proceed!

GLOSSARY

Alban Arthan Welsh name for winter solstice

Alban Eilir Welsh name for spring equinox

Alban Elfed Welsh name for autumn equinox

Alban Hefin Welsh name for summer solstice

Ancient Order of Druids in America (AODA) Druid order founded in 1912 by a group of American Druids

Awen Spirit of creativity and inspiration, the human expression of the One Life

Belteinne (Beltane) Alternate name for Calan Mai

Calan Mai Welsh name for May Day or Belteinne, Celtic fire festival

Calan Gwyngalaf Welsh name for Lammas or Lughnasadh, Celtic fire festival

Calan Myri Welsh name for Candlemas or Imbolc, Celtic fire festival

Calan Tachwedd Welsh name for All Hallows (All Saint's Day or Samhuinn), Celtic fire festival

Cauldron of Air Bowl filled with incense (or potpourri) used in Druidic rituals, symbolizing the air element

Cauldron of Earth Bowl filled with earth or stones used in Druidic rituals, symbolizing the earth element

Cauldron of Fire Bowl with a votive candle (or crystal) inside used in Druidic rituals, symbolizing the fire element

Cauldron of Water Bowl filled with water used in Druidic rituals, symbolizing the water element

Coelbren alphabet Symbolic Druidic alphabet that was either invented or rediscovered by the Welsh poet Iolo Morganwg (1747–1826)

Derw Welsh for "oak"

Derwydd Welsh for "Druid"

Einigan the Giant In Welsh legend, the first of all created beings

Gorseddau Welsh for assemblies or meetings of bards

Gwydd Welsh for "wisdom or knowledge" (-*wydd* when combined with another word)

Gwyddons Wise ones; ancient loremasters of the Celts

Helio-Arkite Theoretically, the oldest religion, believed by some nineteenth-century historians to have been founded by survivors of Noah's flood

Imbolc Alternate name for Candlemas

Lammas August harvest festival; see Calan Gwyngalaf, Lughnasadh

Lughnasadh Alternate name for Lammas

Mabinogion Medieval Welsh narrative collection of early mythological and mystical stories

Mistletoe Sacred holy and healing plant in the Druidic tradition

Nwyfre Druidic Welsh word for the life force or the One Life

Ogham Early Medieval Irish symbolic alphabet

One Life Druidic phrase for "life force," see *nwyfre*

Order of Bards Ovates and Druids (OBOD) Druid order founded in 1964 by Ross Nichols, an English poet and educator

Ritual of the Druid Grove Method of establishing sacred space for a specific purpose and then, once the work is finished, returning the space to its everyday condition

Ritual of the Three Rays A rite of blessing and protection

Samhuinn (Samhain) Alternate name for All Hallows

Solar current The flow of One Life from the Sun

Telluric current The flow of One Life from Earth, or Tellus (Latin for "Earth")

Three rays of light The emblem of Druidry and the symbol of the Druid Revival tradition

RESORCES

ORGANIZATIONS

There are many Druid organizations in the world today. Among the most active and welcoming are these:

The Ancient Order of Druids in America (AODA), http://aoda.org

The Druid Network (TDN), https://druidnetwork.org

The Order of Bards, Ovates, and Druids (OBOD), https://druidry.org

BOOKS

Among the resources that will be most useful to you in your Druid path are books on plants, birds, and other things in nature, and these are specific to the region in which you live   a book on nature in southern New England won't do you a lot of good if you live in Georgia, British Columbia, or Australia! You can find out what nature books about your own region are worth having by talking to local nature clubs and seeing what books are recommended on local nature websites. Among the books more broadly useful for Druids are these:

Billington, Penny, *The Path of Druidry* (Woodbury, MN: Llewellyn, 2011).
A solid introductory guide to the modern Druid tradition from a longtime Druid, well worth reading and study.

Brown Jr., Tom, *Tom Brown's Field Guide to Nature Observation and Tracking* (New York: Berkley, 1983).

———, *Tom Brown's Field Guide to the Forgotten Wilderness* (New York: Berkley, 1987).

Expert tracker and outdoorsman Tom Brown Jr. has written many books about wilderness survival and living with nature. These two are especially useful for the aspiring Druid. The "forgotten wilderness" mentioned in the title of the second book is the one most of us live in—the urban and suburban environments we share with many other living things.

Carr-Gomm, Philip, *Druid Mysteries: Ancient Wisdom for the 21st Century* (London: Rider, 2002).

———, *The Druid Way* (Shaftesbury, UK: Element, 1993).

———, *What Do Druids Believe?* (London: Granta, 2006).

Three good introductions to Druidry by one of the leading figures in the contemporary Druid movement, the former head of the Order of Bards Ovates and Druids.

Carr-Gomm, Philip, ed., *The Druid Renaissance* (London: Thorsons, 1996).

———, *In the Grove of the Druids* (London: Watkins, 2002).

Two valuable anthologies of modern Druid writings. The first is a general anthology of essays by modern Druids, the second is a collection of essays by Carr-Gomm's teacher Ross Nichols. Both have much to offer the student of Druid lore.

Gantz, Jeffrey, trans., *The Mabinogion* (London: Penguin, 1976).

This classic collection of old Welsh legends has been translated into English many times. This is the translation I like best.

Greer, John Michael, *The Dolmen Arch*, 2 volumes (Portland, OR: Azoth, 2020).

———, *The Druid Magic Handbook* (San Francisco, CA: Weiser, 2007).

———, *The Druidry Handbook* (San Francisco, CA: Weiser, 2006).

———, *The Secret of the Temple* (Woodbury, MN: Llewellyn, 2016).

Four books by the author of the present book, three of them on Druidry. *The Druidry Handbook* is aimed at beginners, *The Druid Magic Handbook* is an intermediate book, and *The Dolmen Arch*, a reconstruction of a Druid training course from the 1920s, is fairly advanced. *The Secret of the Temple* is a first exploration of the ancient lore of healing the earth using the two currents, which was mentioned in this book in chapter 5.

Greer, John Michael, ed., *The Druid Revival Reader* (Everett, WA: Starseed, 2011).

As far as I know, this is the only anthology of Druid Revival writings currently in print, covering the tradition from William Stukeley in the 1740s to Ross Nichols in the 1940s.

Gregory, Lady Augusta, *Gods and Fighting Men* (Gerrards Cross, UK: Colin Smythe, 1993).

———, *Cuchulain of Muirthemne* (Gerrards Cross, UK: Colin Smythe, 1993).

There are many good versions of the old Irish myths and legends in English, but these two volumes are among the best. Lady Gregory was a famous collector of Irish folktales and was a fine writer.

Hall, Manly Palmer, *Self-Unfoldment by Disciplines of Realization* (Los Angeles: Philosophical Research Society, 1942).

Hall was one of the most influential spiritual teachers of the twentieth century. This is a valuable guide to meditation and spiritual development, well suited to Druid practice.

Horowitz, Alexandra, *On Looking: A Walker's Guide to the Art of Observation* (New York: Scribners, 2014).

The art of paying attention to what is actually around us is an important part of the Druid path, and this book is a good introduction.

Nichols, Ross, *The Book of Druidry* (London: Thorsons, 1990).

The most influential writer and thinker in the twentieth century Druid movement, Ross Nichols wrote several books. This intriguing guide to the Druid Revival tradition is the only one currently available.

Plotnik, Arthur, *The Urban Tree Book* (New York: Three Rivers Press, 2000).

This handbook of the most common trees in urban and suburban settings is valuable for Druids who want to learn about their local ecosystems.

Rees, Alwyn, and Brinley Rees, *Celtic Heritage: Ancient Tradition in Ireland and Wales* (London: Thames and Hudson, 1961).

A classic account of Celtic myth and legend in its historical context, this book has become standard reading in many Druid organizations.

Spence, Lewis, *The History and Origins of Druidism* (London: Rider & Co., 1949).
———, *The Magic Arts in Celtic Britain* (Minneola, NY: Dover, 1999).
———, *The Minor Traditions of British Mythology* (NY: Arno Press, 1979).
———, *The Mysteries of Britain* (North Hollywood, CA: Newcastle, 1993).

Spence, a well-known anthropologist and also a gifted poet, was an important figure in the early twentieth century Druid movement, and his books were recommended reading in many of the Druid organizations of the last century. They are still well worth reading, even though some of their scholarship is considered outdated at this point.

Tolstoy, Nikolay, *The Quest for Merlin* (Boston, MA: Little, Brown, 1985).

Behind the legends of Merlin, the enchanter, the adviser of King Arthur, stands a historical figure who was very likely one of the last of the ancient Druids. This lively book gathers together everything that is known about him.

Wheelwright, Nathaniel T., and Bernd Heinrich, *The Naturalist's Notebook* (North Adams, MA: Storey, 2017).

A guide to nature observation with a five-year journal attached for your own notes on what you observe, this is a useful tool for Druids.

Williams, Ernest H., Jr., *The Nature Handbook* (New York: Oxford University Press, 2005).

A good general handbook on nature observation.

Williams ab Ithell, J., ed., *The Barddas of Iolo Morganwg* (York Beach, ME: Weiser, 2004).

A vast collection of documents found or created by Iolo Morganwg, finally edited decades after his death by his student John Williams ab Ithel, this has been one of the chief sourcebooks for Druid Revival groups since its original publication in 1962.

Wood, Ernest, *Concentration: An Approach to Meditation* (Wheaton, IL: Quest, 1949).

A classic manual of Western meditation with helpful exercises.

DIVINATION METHODS

There are many methods of divination practiced by Druids today along with the Coelbren alphabet. These are some of the most widely used at present.

Carr-Gomm, Philip and Stephanie, *The Druid Animal Oracle* (London: Connections, 1994).

————, *The Druidcraft Tarot* (London: Connections, 2005).

————, *The Druid Plant Oracle* (New York; St. Martin's Press, 2007).

These are three of the most popular divination decks among Druids today. The Druid Animal Oracle and Druid Plant Oracle use the animals or plants of Celtic legend and tradition as their symbols, while the Druidcraft Tarot is based on the popular Rider-Waite Tarot deck but with a Celtic theme. The cards are beautifully illustrated by Druid artist Will Worthington.

Greer, John Michael, *The Coelbren Alphabet* (Woodbury, MN: Llewellyn, 2017).

The one book in English on the Coelbren oracle, more detailed than the brief account given in this book, with a variety of divination spreads.

McCracken, Chloe, *The Celtic Lenormand Oracle* (New York: US Games, 2015).

An attractive Celtic-themed version of the popular Lenormand deck, also illustrated by Will Worthington.

Mueller, Mickie, *The Voice of the Trees* (Woodfield, MN: Llewellyn, 2011).

A popular Ogham card deck with beautiful illustrations.

Murray, Liz and Colin, *The Celtic Tree Oracle* (New York: St. Martin's Press, 1988).
The most widely used version of the Ogham oracle, with stylized Celtic images painted by Vanessa Card.

O'Driscoll, Dana, *The Plant Spirit Oracle Deck* (Philadelphia, PA: Druid's Garden, 2020).
————, *Tarot of Trees* (Philadelphia, PA: Druid's Garden, 2009).
Two vivid botanical-themed decks by the current head of the Ancient Order of Druids in America.

PICTURE CREDITS

Alamy: Science History Images: 143

ClipArt ETC: 45, 80, 186

Getty Images: *DigitalVision Vectors:* aleksandarvelasevic: 67; bauhaus1000: 18, 177, endpapers; benoitb: 6, 164, 202; duncan1890: vi, 21, 40, 112, 170, 180; GeorgePeters: 37, 49 (forest), 154, 167, 174; ilbusca: 27, 35; Nastasic: 183; *E+:* nicoolay: 190; *iStock/Getty Images Plus:* andipantz: 88; Campwillowlake: 16; cjp: 57; kate_sun: 51; Kreatiw: 148; Man_Half-tube: 109, 116; Paul Art: 93; Pinonova: 98; powerofforever: 83; stournsaeh: 32, 212; thedakfish: 106; ULADZIMIR ZGURSKI: 142; Vladayoung: 149

Internet Archive: 114

Shutterstock.com: agsandrew: 96; artdock: cover, i, 4, 38, 78, 172 (tree and roots); Yulia Buchatskaya: 3, 194; Dear Fashion Design: spine (green man); elfinadesign: cover, i, iii (cross knot); Ezepov Dmitry: 49 (starburst); Gallinago_ media: cover, i(raven); Morphart Creation: 9, 59; mountain beetle: 73, 74, 76, 77; OK-SANA: cover, spine, i, 4, 38, 78, 172 (oak leaves, acorns), throughout (oak leaf border); patrimonio designs ltd: throughout (green man); Sergey Pekar: 85; Vera Petruk: 34; renikca: 117; Maryna Serohina: 17; TabitaZn: cover, i (spiral); TheMumins: cover, i (spider); Mariya Volochek: throughout (Celtic borders); yulianas: cover, i (triple spiral)

Wellcome Collection: 13, 24, 26, 91

Courtesy of Wikimedia Commons: cover, spine, i, 64 (Awen); throughout (rod with pentagram); 43, 91, 146; Internet Archive: 169; National Library of Wales: 29, 103

Courtesy of Yale University: 70

INDEX

Note: Page numbers in **bold** indicate Glossary definitions.

NOTES

NOTES

NOTES

NOTES

NOTES

ABOUT THE AUTHOR

JOHN MICHAEL GREER is one of today's most respected writers and scholars in the fields of occultism, and the award-winning author of more than fifty books, including *The Conspiracy Book* and *The Occult Book*, *The Druidry Handbook*, and *The New Encyclopedia of Natural Magic*. An initiate in Freemasonry, the Hermetic Order of the Golden Dawn, and the Order of Bards, Ovates & Druids, Greer served as the Grand Archdruid of the Ancient Order of Druids in America (AODA) for twelve years. He lives in Rhode Island with his wife, Sara. Greer is also the author of eleven fantasy and science fiction novels and ten nonfiction books on peak oil and the future of industrial society, and also blogs weekly on politics, magic, and the future at www.ecosophia.net.